Dumb Energy

A Critique of Wind and Solar Energy[1]

Norman Rogers

---

[1] Previous published as Dumb Energy: A Rant Against Wind and Solar Energy

Table of Contents

Introduction

Sometimes sweet reason doesn't get the job done. You can wear yourself out sweetly explaining some things. People don't listen. Why should they? They already know everything they want to know. With these types you have to be forceful.

Wind and solar electricity are renewable energy. How nice to pluck energy out of the air and the sky. It's a scam. Big money men and screwball dreamers, otherwise called environmentalists, are cooperating to keep the scam going.

Apparently, it has not dawned on the supporters of the scam that solar does not work at night and wind only works when the wind is blowing. The core characteristic of wind and solar is that these are erratic sources of electricity. The supply is randomly intermittent. Who in hell thinks this dumb energy is a good way to supply electricity?

The wind and solar promoters demand that the grid be reengineered to become a "smart" grid. The idea is that if the grid is smart enough, that will compensate for the dumb wind and solar energy. That's actually what they have in mind. The point of the smart grid is to make the grid more agile, the better to follow the ups and downs of wind and solar.

Wind and solar are unreliable, dangerous to the electrical grid, and far more expensive than conventional sources of electricity. The environmental benefits are non-existent, and the economics only make sense if you think that healthy industries are industries on government welfare.

The numbers are clear, the engineering is clear, and the science is clear. Why is this scam succeeding? Many writers have made the same points I make in this book. Yet, government-subsidized wind and solar installations are still being built.

The obsession with renewable energy distracts from the real problems of the electric grid. The grid is vulnerable to a long-term collapse from sabotage, or even from a natural magnetic storm originating in the sun. Public money should not be spent for a wind and solar environmental fantasy.

This critique is a serious book, filled with facts and numbers.

The Effect of Human Passion

The renewable energy scam survives because some people are making money and because some people have made renewable energy into a religion. The ideologues provide respectability for the profiteers.

A century ago, Vilfredo Pareto, a cynical Italian, in the spirt of Machiavelli, pointed out that men's beliefs are more the result of passion than of logic. His thesis has been proven by events many times. It very much applies to wind and solar renewable energy. No matter the facts, people, inspired by passion, believe in wind and solar energy. The most important supporters of renewable energy are members of the intellectual classes, ignorant concerning accounting or engineering, yet enamored by renewable energy.

Extracting energy from wind and sunlight is a seductive theory. But, the theory is impractical. The installations are too expensive. The power produced is erratic, changing with the comings and goings of the wind and sun. Erratic power saves fuel in fossil fuel plants when it arrives, but it does not displace investment in fossil fuel plants. Those plants must still be present as backup for the erratic power.

The renewable energy industry is financed by government subsidies and sweetheart deals that are hidden from consumers.

The over-educated, intellectual mind values an elegant theory over a messy reality. The result is tension between ivory tower thinkers and practical men working in the trenches of the economy. The practical men easily see the weaknesses in abstract theories, weaknesses that are invisible to the ivory tower thinkers. But the practical men are not equipped to assert or defend their reality in political, media or academic circles. If they try, they are patronized and ignored. A seductive theory trumps pedestrian and annoying facts in the intellectual mind. For this reason, ridiculously impracticable renewable energy finds wide support in circles populated by thinkers accustomed to mobilizing the power of the state to promote impractical ideas with the taxpayers' money. For these thinkers, ideology comes first. Evidence that contradicts ideology must be bad evidence. Evidence to support ideological positions is manufactured as necessary.

In a similar context, the climate scientist, Richard Lindzen, remarked that data that challenges the global warming hypothesis are simply changed.[2] Real climate data is complicated and can be "reinterpreted" rather than blatantly falsified. Like global warming, renewable energy also suffers from faked data in support of intellectually seductive ideas. Fakery happens whenever the price of wind or solar electricity is announced without disclosing the massive subsidies. The fake claims of the proselytizers of renewable energy gives the public the impression that wind and solar are commercially competitive. Informed opposition to the wind and solar industry is marginalized and rarely gets a hearing before the larger public. That's because the informed opposition is citing messy and boring facts rather than a romantic and appealing theory.

---

[2] Climate Science: Is it Currently Designed to Answer Questions? Richard Lindzen. Euresis Journal Winter 2012.

Arguing facts with a believer in renewable energy is generally futile. Their belief is not based on facts, but based on passion. Rarely will a serious believer change his mind because he is presented with facts. Fortunately, most people are not true believers, but victims of constant propaganda. One can plant a seed of doubt in such persons by presenting facts. It is often helpful to point out that birds are sliced up by wind turbines.

The Populist Enemies of Wind Turbines

Groups of rural residents are furious at having wind farms foisted on them. They object to having landscapes they treasure contaminated by massive windmills. They object to the whump-whump noise and the flickering shadows. Some of those groups advance beyond their esthetic objections to exposing the full scope of the scam.

Greg Hubner, a resident of South Dakota wrote: *Paradise Destroyed: The Destruction of Rural Living by the Wind Farm Scam*. His book is rooted in deep knowledge gained from the political fight against wind farm developers in South Dakota. He wrote the following:

> Powerful corporations and politicians have legislated their way to wealth by passing laws for their own financial benefit. Wind energy is a prime example. Instead of capitalism and a true "free market" where the state simply acts as a referee to establish a level playing field, the government is hi-jacked through politics to hinder competitors and give select businesses an unfair advantage.

Hubner's analysis is correct. His book covers much of the ground that will be covered here, and the ground covered by other opponents of wind power. But, Hubner makes the mistake of giving credit to renewable energy as a concept sound in theory, but faulty in practice. He weakens his argument by conceding the high ground to the windmill developers. Renewable energy is not good in theory but flawed in execution. Rather, the theory driving the entire industry is flawed.

Wind Turbines Palm Springs, CA

Fallacies of Renewable Energy

The idea of renewable energy as a reliable, comprehensive solution to future energy needs is an error, resting on these faulty assumptions:

1) We will run out of fossil fuels in the foreseeable future.
2) Burning fossil fuels is dangerous to health and inevitably creates ugly contamination of the atmosphere.
3) Renewable energy is financially competitive.
4) Carbon dioxide emissions will create a climate disaster.

These dubious assumptions will be disputed in this book.

As a practical matter, renewable energy is mainly wind electricity and solar electricity. In the U.S. over $100 billion has been spent on heavily subsidized wind turbines and a lesser amount on solar electricity. The aspiration of the industry and its supporters is to greatly increase that spending. Ultimately, if the promoters have their way, our electric rates will double or triple as they have in certain European countries.

This book presents facts to counter the massive propaganda promoting renewable energy. The propaganda comes from government agencies, the media, environmental pressure groups, and scientific associations. These groups are shirking their responsibility to present careful and factual analysis. There are honorable exceptions to renewable energy group think. At times the Wall Street Journal runs articles critical of renewable energy. The skeptic ranks are strengthened by some think tanks, intelligent politicians, and numerous scientists and engineers.

Wind generates electricity when the wind blows, and the sun generates electricity when the sun shines. Adding wind or solar to the conventional electric grid imposes adaptation costs. The grid has to be reengineered and operated differently in order to accommodate the erratic nature of wind and solar electricity. The more wind and solar there is, the greater the adaptation cost. The sudden arrival or sudden departure of thousands of megawatts of electricity, according the mood of the wind or the clouds, stresses a grid that was designed to operate in a more sedate and predictable manner.

The promoters of wind and solar have successfully spread the idea that wind and solar are cheaper than traditional sources of energy like fossil fuels, nuclear and hydro. They don't mention the direct government subsidies that cover 30 percent to 50 percent of the cost. They forget to mention the indirect subsidy of "tax equity financing," the special tax deals that allow highly profitable companies to reduce their taxes by providing investment capital to wind and solar projects.

There are "renewable portfolio" laws enacted in many states that guarantee wind and solar a certain fraction of the electricity market. Those laws force utilities to pay high prices in long term contracts for wind and solar electricity. By law and contract the operators of the electrical grid are, in most cases, required, to accept all the wind and solar offered, guaranteeing a lucrative market. The total effect of the privileged position of wind and solar is that taxpayers and electricity consumers are forced to pay for vastly over-priced electricity. The billions of dollars extracted are invisibly submerged in larger flows of taxes and electricity tariffs. It is very hard to find out what utilities are paying for renewable energy. Public utility commissions keep these power purchase agreements secret on the pretense that it is confidential competitive information. It is also information deeply embarrassing to the renewable energy industry.

Wind and solar promoters make it appear that renewable power is cheaper by "forgetting" to mention the subsidies, but also by comparing the cost of electricity at the plant fences – that is the cost of the electricity exiting the plant. Comparing electricity cost at the plant fence ignores the costs imposed on the grid outside of the plant fence by wind or solar. Even by the plant fence comparison, wind and solar can only be made to seem competitive by ignoring the subsidies. But wind and solar also impose ancillary costs on the electrical grid beyond the cost at the plant fence. Because wind and solar are erratic sources of power, the grid has to maintain an agile backup capability to step in when wind or solar waxes and wanes. Not only does this mean that wind and solar can't replace a significant part of the capital investment in the existing grid, but that the existing grid has to be reengineered to increase agility to respond quickly to the comings and goings of renewable power.

The construction of wind and solar generating plants should be stopped immediately. The plants are unreliable, undermine the electrical grid, and generate electricity at a cost vastly greater than the traditional alternatives. But for many proponents of renewable energy, increased costs might be worth it if renewable energy has substantial environmental benefits. Those supposed benefits are illusory.

The Global Warming Justification

Subsidizing wind and solar is often justified on the ground that wind and solar don't emit carbon dioxide, and thus help prevent global warming. Global warming is based on dubious computer projections contradicted by the Earth's climate trends. The evidence is overwhelming that the global warming scare is scientifically flawed. Carbon dioxide is a harmless gas that helps plants grow.[3] It may well influence the climate, but the evidence is that the effect of CO_2 is small, and probably beneficial due to improving the growth of plants.

---

[3] See the website of *The CO2 Coalition* for more on the benefits of CO_2.

Global warming alarmism is fading in the public mind, and is now nothing more than an elite, Western concern. An ABC network poll of the 15 problems that American worry about a great deal ranked climate change at the bottom of the list with 25 percent of respondents reporting that they worry about climate change. In the My World Poll commissioned by the United Nations, climate change was dead last among 16 global concerns, just below phone and Internet access. Only in wealthy countries was climate change anything other than the least concerning issue. But, the promoters of global warming, anxious to manipulate politicians, cite polls that claim that the public is very concerned about global warming or climate change. Polls are easily influenced by the way in which questions are asked, resulting in our polls and their polls.

Global Warming Drama on Central Park West

It's clear that there is no looming climate catastrophe bought on by CO_2 and other so-called greenhouse gases. The computer climate models that make these predictions are deeply flawed. But, the arguments here don't depend on the reader agreeing with or disputing global warming alarmism. Even a true believer in global warming should see that windmills and solar farms are not justified on global warming grounds. If you want to prevent CO_2 emissions there are much more effective and less expensive methods than wind or solar energy: planting trees or utilizing carbon-free nuclear or hydroelectric energy.

Global warming is promoted by self-interested scientists. The idea that scientists are disinterested big thinkers pontificating from on high is not to be taken seriously. Like any other interest group, scientists are susceptible to pursuing self-interest at the expense of the public interest. In his farewell address, President Eisenhower warned against the capture of public policy by a scientific elite dependent on government money. Eisenhower's worst fears have come true. Global warming alarmism has become official government policy, at least under Obama.

For certain scientific groups, green ideas and global warming alarmism are the geese that lay golden eggs. The golden eggs are not just money, but also prestige. Scientists, particularly climate scientists, benefit from global warming alarmism. They are reluctant, individually or as a group, to express skepticism or to critically examine the theories behind global warming alarmism. Peer pressure to conform is so great, that to contradict the group think is heresy, and likely professional suicide. Global warming has transformed climate scientists, formerly nerdy grinds toiling in an obscure corner of academia, into celebrity scientists. The pull of stardom and money has thoroughly corrupted the scientific work.

To better understand the motivations of the scientists, particularly the senior scientists with large budgets and many employees, consider the following. Computer climate models are a logical approach to analyzing the Earth's climate and predicting the future climate – if they work! Developing these models ended up costing hundreds of millions, or even billions. Large numbers of scientists and other technical people made their careers working on the models. But the models don't work, at least not very well. Models from different modeling groups differ, one model to another, by a factor of two to one in temperature projections. The scientists could say to the government that the approach is a failure, close down the labs and fire the employees. That would be the honest approach. But, as Ronald Reagan said: "The closest thing to eternal life on Earth is a government program." So, instead, the climate modelers say, every year, that things are improving and perhaps ask for more money in next year's budget. The political nature of the Intergovernmental Panel on Climate Change, the most important scientific authority on global warming, is shown by its refusal to meaningfully compare the quality of the dozens of climate models it uses to make predictions. Picking one climate model over another would threaten the budgets of the losers and start a bureaucratic war among the modeling organizations that are living off government money. It would become obvious that the modeling idea is a failure if the various labs started fighting with each other.

If global warming is not a serious threat, why spend millions on climate modeling? Naturally, the scientific community continues to loudly claim that global warming is a threat, no matter evidence to the contrary. The skeptics are as welcome as the proverbial skunk at a garden party. The skeptics are effectively told that if they hurt funding, the climate establishment will make them an offer they can't refuse. The offer may be an offer of unemployment. The skeptics excite passions in those with threatened budgets. The scientist Ben Santer was quoted in an email as saying: "Next time I see Pat Michaels at a scientific meeting, I'll be tempted to beat the crap out of him. Very tempted." Pat Michaels is well known as a scientist with skeptical thoughts concerning global warming. Ben Santer, by the way, received a $500,000 MacArthur foundation "genius" prize, an example how sweet life can be if you predict global warming disaster.

Climate modeling is not the only big climate program energized by global warming alarmism. There are people drilling holes in the Arctic and Antarctic ice caps. There are research ships cruising the oceans. There are satellites and underwater robots talking to the satellites. These programs, including even climate modeling, have scientific interest, but the scale of the research has been multiplied many times by the global warming scare campaign compared to what is justified as a purely scientific effort. The vast sums drawn into climate science have inevitably lowered the quality of the research, and of the researchers, under the impetus of rapid expansion. Increasing scientific budgets does not proportionally increase the number of people available with the talent and interest to be good scientists.

Discovering an impending catastrophe is a way for scientists to get attention and research grants. As a consequence, we are deluged with a parade of impending catastrophes that never materialize. When one catastrophe dies of over-exposure, it is replaced by a new impending catastrophe. Global warming will die slowly due to the vast size of the enterprise and the vested interests. When global warming dies, look for ocean acidification to be the replacement impending catastrophe. The belief that the ocean is filled with pieces of plastic floating around is another impending catastrophe that has been getting lots of traction.

The voices of the sincere scientists that object to global warming alarmism are hard to hear over the loud propaganda machine operated by the promoters of global warming. The global warming scientific establishment has many tools for punishing dissenters. Skeptical scientists who cannot be fired, because they have tenure or civil service protection, become objects of ridicule and victims of whispering campaigns.[4]

Risks to the Electric Grid

It's easy to be complacent about the electric grid. It always just works, except for occasional blips. But this complacency is ill-advised: the electrical grid is vulnerable, and renewable energy is increasing that vulnerability.

The effects of a long-term failure of the grid would dwarf those of any hurricane, nor'easter, or flood. The survival of millions would be at risk. Solar storms are caused by explosions on the sun that eject particles toward the Earth. A major solar superstorm, such as occurred in 1859, has the potential to destroy the grid's critical large transformers. These storms can distort the Earth's magnetic field, inducing dangerous currents in long power lines. In the 1859 storm, telegraph lines suffered damage, but there was no electrical grid, back then, to worry about. A 1989 solar storm collapsed the Quebec electrical grid and caused the destruction of a large transformer at a nuclear plant in New Jersey. These storms are random—but as a statistical probability, it is just a matter of time.

Finally, our electrical grid is vulnerable to human, rather than natural attacks. Our most unpredictable and dangerous enemies, Iran and North Korea, understand that is possible to seriously cripple the electric grid by means of an electromagnetic pulse created by a small nuclear device detonated in near outer space—a flash in the sky, killing no one

---

[4] See the youtube interview of Judith Curry:
https://www.bing.com/videos/search?q=judith+curry&&view=detail&mid=D5B9603EDB5B A80A698ED5B9603EDB5BA80A698E&&FORM=VRDGAR

and causing no obvious damage. Such an attack has the potential to destroy capital equipment over a huge area, especially critically important transformers that would take years to replace. The transformers can be protected, but no one is bothering to do that.

Hacking is another way our enemies can harm the electrical grid. The Russians demonstrated this during the war with the Ukraine. By hacking it is possible to destroy capital equipment by short circuiting massive energy flows against the equipment. Transformers and generators can be made to catch on fire via hacking.

Damage to the grid by electromagnetic pulse or sabotage is competing with renewable energy as a priority that demands investment in the grid. Because renewable energy has commanded most of the attention and money, the very real threat to the grid by electromagnetic pulse or sabotage is being neglected.

A fundamental fallacy is that cost is the most important thing to worry about when it comes to the delivery of electricity. Not so, reliability and resilience are far more important, because the cost to the economy of an extended blackout dwarfs the cost of providing electricity. In an extreme case millions of Americans would die from a grid collapse.

The Dysfunction of Environmentalism

The business plan of the major environmental organizations is based on the exaggeration of environmental threats. The global warming scare is the most important current exaggeration. Wind and solar energy are promoted because they don't emit CO_2 and because the environmentalists imagine they can be substituted for most current sources of electricity. The environmentalists only care about man made environmental threats. They need a villain, usually a corporation, to make their cartoon-like stories more dramatic. Natural threats, such as floods, a solar superstorm or a tsunami, are low priority concerns. As nature-worshipers, they can't make nature into the villain. Preventing construction of a dam is more important to the environmentalists than protecting thousands of people from being killed and losing their property in floods. The Sierra

Club's relentless opposition to a high dam on the American River to protect the city of Sacramento, California, is a case in point.

The Sierra Club and similar outfits ran alarmist campaigns against hydroelectric power and nuclear power in the 1970's and 80's, continuing to this day. They don't like hydroelectricity because they hate dams. Environmentalists have a romantic attachment to free-flowing rivers. One would think that the Sierra Club would like nuclear power, given that it is CO_2-free and pollution-free. But the group is hysterically opposed to nuclear power. Policy at the Sierra Club is a collection of childish prejudices rather than a logical structure.

As early as May, 1977, at the tail end of the 70's global cooling scare and in the infancy of the global warming scare, the Sierra Club Bulletin contained this statement:

> A more realistic approach to a sustainable-energy society is to gradually decentralize the energy supply system by utilizing small-scale solar, wind and bioconversion technologies.[5]

When that statement was made, wind and solar were vastly more expensive than they are now, but even then, the Sierra Club embraced the idea of wind and solar. The group's opinions tend to the romantic rather than the practical.

In April 1975, the Sierra Club Bulletin said this about nuclear energy:

> Our society persists in stumbling about on the dark side of exponential energy demand, trifling with atomic poisoning and gambling with the future of 1,333[6] generations of our descendants, not to mention all of life itself.

---

[5] Bioconversion is making products from waste and renewable resources.
[6] The reason for the number 1,333 is a mystery.

Vastly more people die in coal mines every year than have died in the entire history of the nuclear power industry.[7] The idea that nuclear power will create mutations in the human genome is inconsistent with the fact that radiation exposure from natural sources dwarfs, by orders of magnitude, exposure from nuclear power.

The environmental lobby has boxed itself in with past alarmist campaigns against dams and nuclear power. Hydro and nuclear are logical ways to get CO_2-free power. They are a logical step in the crusade to reduce the supposed global warming. But, the environmental organizations cannot damage their credibility by changing their position on hydro and nuclear. Instead they support wind and solar technology; technology that is ineffective, either for generating electricity or for reducing CO_2 emissions. (A few prominent greens, such as James Hansen and Steward Brand, do support nuclear power.)

The environmental movement is detached from economic and engineering realities. The movement traffics in impracticable and romantic ideas that will encourage naive supporters to write checks. The voice of the critics is muted by the media's leftist orientation and the media's love of sensationalism. Evil corporations that must be resisted are part of the sales pitch. Any critic of environmental dogma is attacked as a tool of capitalist interests. Environmental organizations are hostile to capitalism and friendly to government regulation.

The environmental non-profits have a big business of suing government and industry to extract settlements in return for not obstructing projects. We should ask why law is structured so as to allow obstructive lawsuits bought for the purpose of blackmail.

Renewable Portfolio Laws

About 30 U.S. states have passed laws requiring that some percentage of their electricity come from "renewable" sources, mainly wind and solar. The main beneficiaries of these laws are

---

[7] BBC News: http://www.bbc.com/news/world-latin-america-11533349 -- Estimate 12,000 deaths from mining each year. Nuclear reactors by comparison are only responsible for a handful of deaths: http://www.world-nuclear.org/information-library/safety-and-security/safety-of-plants/safety-of-nuclear-power-reactors.aspx

not the public—which pays more for electricity—but green energy companies and their investors, who are being made rich at the public's expense.

As a result of these laws, utilities are forced to pay high prices and sign long term power purchase agreements with developers of wind and solar power. But utilities don't care about these exorbitant prices, so long as they are allowed to pass them on to electricity consumers. The sweetheart contracts, and various subsidies, make it possible for wind and solar companies to finance their projects. These companies are supporters of the politicians who enact renewable portfolio laws in the first place — a perpetual cycle that costs consumers at every step.

An example of a sweetheart contract in California is the power purchase agreement between the Ivanpah solar plant and the Pacific Gas and Electric Company. The contract was secret for three years. The price of electricity in that contract is more than 14 cents per kilowatt hour, about three times what wholesale electricity from a natural gas plant would cost. Besides the generous contract terms, the Ivanpah plant was built with extensive government subsidies.

Green Ideologues and Nature Worship

For the green ideologues, the idea that burning fossil fuels will cause a climate catastrophe is appealing. The looming climate catastrophe provides an excuse to insist on a complete revamping of the energy economy. That leads to changing everything about how people work and live. Telling people how to live is common to ideological and utopian mass movements. Crusades, no matter if wrong-headed, inspire and give meaning to life. Young people, especially, fall for utopian crusades.

Green ideologues use their ideology as a route to political and economic power. The totalitarian impulse is strong among the green ideologues. They feel entitled to impose their ideas on the rest of us. Though the evidence is overwhelming that the Earth is more resilient than the green ideologues want us to believe, they portray the Earth as a victim that must be protected by the imposition of utopian green ideas.

Green ideology has an element of nature worship. It assumes that the Earth is sacred and that the Earth is in danger from

Introduction

man. This is the opposite of the Judeo-Christian ideology that – whether or not one is religious – remains the historic basis of our civilization. In the Book of Genesis, God says to mankind: "Be fruitful and increase in number; fill the earth and subdue it. Rule over the fish in the sea and the birds in the sky and over every living creature that moves on the ground." Subduing the Earth and filling the Earth with people is about as far from the ideology of the Sierra Club as one can get. The Sierra Club and fellow green ideologues may think that nature worship is something new. But, plenty of illiterate peoples living in jungles are a step ahead of the Sierra Club.

When a paradise on Earth fails to emerge from the adoption of utopian ideas, totalitarianism often follows. Rather than changing their ideas, because they prove ineffective, ideologues double down and try to force their ideas on the population. That, of course, is the history of communism. The green ideologues in the U.S. are not communists. Rather than championing the workers, they champion the Earth. They also champion themselves.

The Economic Argument

This chapter outlines the economic case against wind and solar. We compute the cost of electricity at the plant fence, providing examples for wind, solar and natural gas. But the cost at the plant fence is only part of the story. The grid, as it exists before wind and solar is introduced, is not displaced by wind and solar. Wind and solar are nearly useless appendages added to the grid. Wind and solar are erratic generators, so the grid, as it was before wind and solar, has to remain in place to provide electricity when wind and solar are "sleeping." Storage of electricity is the holy grail that the advocates of wind and solar are seeking because it would smooth the erratic generation of wind and solar. But, that holy grail has not been found because all the methods of storing electricity are too expensive, or otherwise unsuited to the need.

Wind and sunshine have been used for generations as a source of energy. Windmills on the American great plains have been, and still are, used to pump water from wells for cattle. Non-electrical solar heat collectors are used to heat swimming pools. Living plants use sunshine to power photosynthesis, the process that allows plants to create plant bodies from carbon dioxide taken from the air and water sucked out of the ground.

Some Terminology

Electric grid – There are 3 major grids in the U.S. – Western, Eastern and Texas. Electricity is provided by dozens of synchronized and interconnected generating plants in each grid.

Watt, kilowatt, megawatt – A watt is a rate of energy flow. A 100-watt light bulb receives an energy flow of 100 watts when it is turned on. A kilowatt is 1000 watts and a megawatt 1,000,000 watts.

Kilowatt hour (kWh) and megawatt hour (MWh) – A quantity of energy. A kilowatt hour is the amount of energy from the flow of one kilowatt for one hour. Residential electricity usage is billed as so many cents per kWh. In many states you might pay 10 cents per kWh. In California it might be 40 cents. A megawatt hour is 1000 times bigger.

Solar power – The preferred method of generating electricity from the sun is by solar cells, semiconductor devices that absorb sunlight and generates electricity. An alternate and more expensive method, thermal solar, generates heat by optically concentrating sunlight with mirrors and using the heat to make steam that drives a turbine.

Wind power – A wind turbine, that looks like an airplane propeller is turned by the wind and drives a generator that generates electricity.

In each of those examples there is a storage or accumulation mechanism for the product of energy. Water pumped by wind is stored in a tank. Heat from thermal solar collectors is stored in the water of the swimming pool. Plant bodies created by photosynthesis are accumulated as the plants grow. The fact that the wind may not blow, or the sun may not shine at unpredictable times is not a problem, because the product generated is accumulated in a storage medium. Except in marginal cases, the electrical grid does not store electricity. Generation and consumption have to be well–balanced. So, the erratic nature of wind and solar is a problem. The grid has to scramble to find electricity from someplace else if the wind dies or a cloud obscures the sun.

Electricity in the modern electrical grid is overwhelmingly generated at the same time it is consumed. If there were a way to store massive amounts of electricity, at a reasonable cost, the erratic nature of wind and solar electricity could be smoothed out, storing electricity when generation is strong and releasing the stored electricity when generation is weak.

There are ways to store electricity but they all have problems that preclude adoption on the scale necessary[8]. Most people think of batteries, but batteries are extremely expensive, and most types of batteries wear out quickly. Batteries have specialized applications for very short-term storage of electricity that can be accessed quickly.

Herdecke Pumped Storage Plant Germany 153 megawatts 4 hours at full power 75% efficiency

Alamy

Pumped storage is the traditional system for storing large amounts of electricity. It requires two reservoirs of water at different altitudes connected by a reversible hydroelectric generator. Water is pumped uphill to store electricity and stored water runs downhill through a turbine to generate electricity.

---

[8] The Energy Storage Association has much useful information on their website: energystorage.org

A pumped storage plant requires building a specialized hydroelectric plant. That is expensive. Pumped storage requires a good site in mountainous terrain; something that is not available in many parts of the country. Long power lines from the wind or solar installation to the pumped storage site are expensive and lose part of the electricity due to the electrical resistance of the line. Thirty percent of the electricity could easily be lost using pumped storage to smooth the flow of wind and solar electricity. The cost of the electricity could be doubled or tripled, due to the capital cost of pumped storage and energy losses in the system.

Because storage of electricity from wind or solar is not economic, the alternative that has emerged is that the "rest of the grid," the part that is not wind or solar, has to accommodate the erratic flows of wind or solar electricity.

The usual relationship between grid operation and wind or solar power plants is that the grid is obliged to accept all the wind or solar energy that can be generated, even if it is inconvenient. That relationship is imposed by politics. Fossil fuel plants, in contrast, are "dispatchable." That means that the grid operators tell the plants when to generate and when not to generate. Only in extremis, can the grid operators tell the politically privileged wind or solar to shut down. Often the power purchase agreement requires that the wind and solar companies be paid for electricity they can't generate because a curtailment has been ordered. This tail wagging the dog relationship is a consequence of the political power of the owners and promoters of renewable energy. If the wind and solar were dispatched on the same terms as fossil fuel plants, wind and solar would be more hopelessly uneconomic than they already are. Potential power generation is lost forever when a wind or solar plant is required to shut down when it could have been generating electricity.

Accommodating wind and solar requires that the massive generating plants that compromise the rest of the grid be throttled up and down as the wind or solar power output changes. That way, electricity supply and demand can be kept in balance. The balance does not have to be exact, because within a limited range the grid is self-balancing. If some users start using more power, that power is stolen from other users who will use less power. But for large shifts in power consumption, generation must be increased or decreased to match supply with demand.

The generating plants that compose the traditional electric grid are massive machines. They can't be throttled up and down on demand like a car. Too fast changes in power output result in temperature gradients stressing the machinery. Large fossil fuel or nuclear plants often take many hours to start up. A major generator may weigh hundreds of tons. Typically, the armature spins at 3600 revolutions per minute and a hydrogen atmosphere is maintained inside the generator to reduce air friction on the spinning armature. A coal plant might consume 300 tons of coal per hour, or 160 pounds per second. The coal is typically ground to a powder by huge grinders before it is burned. These generating plants are not friendly to rapid start and stop operation.

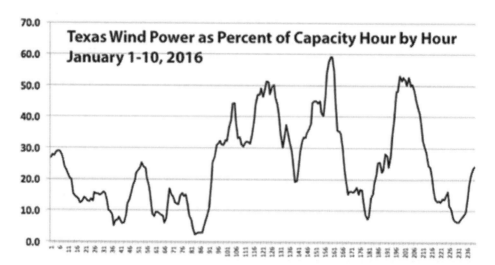

An example from Texas illustrates the problem. Texas has a large, 18,000-megawatt, wind generation system, mostly in west Texas. Hour by hour output for 10-days of the Texas wind system is shown in the graph.[9] Swings in wind power of 30% or 5,000 megawatts in a few hours are not unusual. A swing of 5,000 megawatts is an amount of power that would require five large coal or nuclear plants to generate, or enough electricity to provide average consumption for 4 million homes. Wind power

[9] Ercot: Hourly Aggregated Wind Output
The Economic Argument

is inherently volatile. The power generated is proportional to the cube of the wind velocity. The way the math works is that a 10% decline in wind velocity results in a 30% decline in power generated. Volatility in the wind is amplified in the power output.

The power grid and its equipment were not designed with the expectation of introducing large quantities of erratic power. The political power of the wind and solar proponents forces the issue. The grid operators are adapting the best they can.

The Rest of the Grid Must Stand Alone

Because wind and solar can't be counted on, the "rest of the grid" has to be able to stand alone, or very close to alone. To be clear: if wind and solar vanished overnight, the grid would get along perfectly well. Adding wind and solar to the grid does not replace any significant part of the existing grid because the existing grid must be ready to step in when wind or solar is generating little electricity.

Accounts frequently appear in the press that give the impression that wind or solar can replace fossil fuel generation. This would only be true if the wind and solar had a high probability of being available, particularly during times of high demand. According to a year-long, hour by hour record of wind output for the Texas grid, in 2016, wind generation fell to as little as 0.8% of installed capacity. That happened on August 31, 2016 at noon. At that time the total demand was 54,000 megawatts, quite a bit less than the all-time high demand of 71,000 megawatts. However, if this near zero wind generation took place when demand was close to the all-time high, it would be essential to have enough other resources to power the grid without wind.

California has a very reliable summer solar generation because California has a great deal of sunshine and practically no rain in the summer. Solar vanishes when the sun sets, but close to peak grid consumption continues well into the evening. On September 1, 2017 California experienced an all-time peak load of a little over 50,000 megawatts, between 4 p.m. and 6 p.m. By 6 p.m. two thirds of solar generation had been lost. By 7 p.m. 90% of solar generation was lost, but demand had only decreased from 50,000 to 48,000 megawatts. By 8 p.m. all the solar generation was lost but demand was still over 46,000 megawatts. It seems unlikely that solar can replace any significant part of the rest of the grid, because solar turns off too soon in the evening. The demand after 7 p.m. has to be met by traditional generators.

There is a type of solar plant that can store energy in the form of heat in a tank of molten salt and then use that heat to generate electricity after the sun sets. The problem is that these *thermal solar plants* are far more expensive than the common photovoltaic plants and the electricity generated costs double or triple.

"Green Power" plant near Palm Springs, CA 22, 750-kW turbines. Installed 1999.

Even in California there are times when summer solar is compromised by cloudy weather. On August 2, 2017, total utility-scale solar generation declined by half due to monsoon tropical weather hitting Southern California. At the same time demand was high, probably due to a combination of high humidity, increasing air conditioning load and a correlated reduction in residential, rooftop, solar output, increasing apparent residential consumption. As a result, thermal natural gas generation had to be extensively mobilized.

Whether wind or solar can replace any of the rest of the grid resources becomes a statistical question. During times of stress there is some probability that solar or wind will be working, so in theory some traditional generation could be abandoned, hoping that wind or solar will fill the hole when there is a stressful situation. This probably doesn't work very well for solar because the stressful time tends to be at the same time the sun is setting.

An additional factor is that rest of the grid has to be deployed to provide balancing regulation to handle rapid shifts in wind or solar. As wind or solar becomes more significant, more investment in modifications to the traditional grid are needed to supply agility. We don't try to estimate that expense in our cost estimates. Instead, we assume that adding wind or solar does not increase or decrease the capital investment in traditional generation. Our assumption is that, due to the erratic nature of wind or solar, the wind or solar is an appendage to the grid, not a replacement for grid capital investment.

The photo below shows a combination of a gas turbine and a large battery developed by General Electric and installed by Southern California Edison. This unit is an example of how introducing wind or solar creates a need for new equipment and new investment in the rest of the grid. By combining a battery and a gas turbine the combination is far more agile than the turbine by itself. The unit can start delivering power immediately while the gas turbine is ramping up, a process that might take 10 minutes. The unit is able to ramp output up and down more quickly with less thermal stress on the turbine to match the variations in renewable power. The battery does not carry the load for long periods, but rather buffers ramp up and ramp down episodes of the gas turbine.

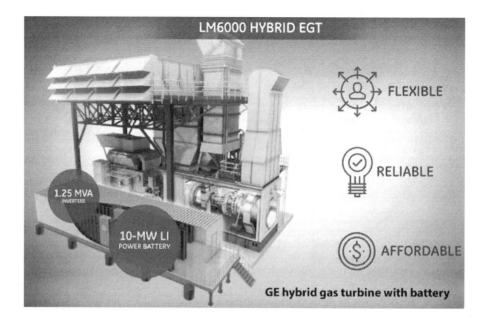

GE hybrid gas turbine with battery

The Cost of Substituting Wind or Solar for Traditional Power

On average, the sources of electricity in 2017 in the U.S. are as follows:

Natural Gas	32%
Coal	30%
Nuclear	20%
Hydropower	7.5%
Wind	6.3%
Solar	1.3%
Other	3%

Many states have renewable portfolio standards that require them to increase the percentage of renewable energy in their mix. Nationally, wind and solar provide 7.6% of electricity, but with wide geographical variation. Many states want to increase their renewable energy by 10% or 20% of consumption. California has a target that renewable energy should be 50% of consumption.

When renewable energy is being generated some other form of energy has to be curtailed. The logical energy to curtail is natural gas. That's because natural gas is the most agile for following the ups and downs of wind or solar. Hydro is also agile, but overall is a minor contributor and often seasonal. We have already established that introducing renewable results in the removal of essentially no existing power plants, because the renewable energy is erratic and cannot be counted on to substitute for conventional plants. If one were to claim, for example, based on a probability calculation, that 10% of natural gas power generation could be abandoned if some amount of renewable energy were added, it would not make much difference in our economic analysis.

Nationally, combined cycle natural gas, the main natural gas technology, has an average capacity factor of very close to 50%. A 50% capacity factor means that the plants generate only half the power they could if they ran at full capacity all the time. The average capacity factor is only 50% because gas is used to follow the ups and downs of the daily electricity consumption cycle. Most gas plants are throttled back late night when electricity use is low. Nuclear, coal and sometimes hydro, tend to be operated at a constant output, leaving it to gas to increase output to handle daytime peaks or follow the variations in wind or solar energy.

A natural gas generating plant has both fixed and variable costs. The fixed cost includes capital cost amortized over the assumed life of the plant and the fixed costs of operation, such as the staff salaries. The variable cost, mainly fuel, depends on the amount of electricity generated. The cost of fuel is about 2 cents per kWh for efficient plants at current gas prices.

When wind or solar is generating electricity, gas plants are throttled back, saving 2 cents for every kWh of electricity not generated by gas. Those kWh's are replaced by kWh's generated by wind or solar. The fixed costs associated with gas continue unabated with the addition of wind or solar.

Detailed Comparison, Cost of Wind, Solar and Natural Gas Electricity

This section presents results that are supported by detailed information in Appendix 1. The cost of generating electricity, measured at the plant fence, is given for wind, solar and natural gas. The cost given here is a simplified cost, without subsidies, that assumes zero profit and neglects minor expenses. A zero-profit cost is called the levelized cost of energy (LCOE). Add about 15% to the simplified LCOE cost to get a more real-world cost including a reasonable profit. The cost of fuel is included in the 4.88 cent per kWh price for natural gas electricity.

Simplified Cost of Various Generating Technologies			
	Wind	Solar Photovoltaic	Natural Gas
Cost Cents per kWh Plant Fence	7.27	7.76	4.88
Cost of Fuel Cents per kWh			2.2
Subsidy Cents Per kWh	5.1	5.6	

Because the only economic contribution of wind or solar is the savings in fuel at the backup gas plants, the total subsidy for wind or solar is the cost of the wind or solar less the savings in fuel. The subsidy is the amount that wind or solar has to be subsidized to be competitive with natural gas. The subsidy is financed by a combination of direct subsidies and higher per kWh rates charged the utility that buys the wind or solar power. These numbers are typical values and will be different for atypical situations. For example, in some places the backup plants might be hydro instead of natural gas. In that case water, rather than fuel might be saved when wind or solar is generating and it would be necessary to assign a cost to the water. (If the hydro backup plant has plenty of water, then a wind or solar plant is a waste of money, because one could just run the hydro plant and dispense with the wind or solar plant.) In our comparisons, we are neglecting the lower utilization of gas plants used as backup plants. Lower utilization (capacity factor) increases the cost per kWh of electricity generated by the gas plants due to the capital cost being spread over fewer kWh's.

The numbers in the table are based on costs published by the National Renewable Energy laboratory. These costs will vary considerably depending on the assumed capacity factor, the cost of fuel, etc. In the real world, for wind, the capacity factor tends to be about 35% under typical circumstances. For solar 19% is typical. My cost calculation is based on an assumed project life of 25 years and a discount rate (like interest rate) of 8%. An inflation rate for labor of 2% a year is assumed. Zero inflation rate is assumed for the cost of natural gas, given the downward trend in the cost of natural gas. These are realistic values and similar to values used by other authorities. Further details are in Appendix 1.

The Explicit and Hidden Subsidies for Wind and Solar

As shown by the table above, every kWh generated by wind or solar requires a subsidy of about 5 cents. There are explicit and hidden subsidies. For wind the explicit federal subsidy, or production tax credit, is 2.4 cents per kWh for the first 10-years. That subsidy is indexed for inflation. For solar there is an explicit subsidy of 30% of the capital cost by way of a tax credit. (This is a simplified discussion of the explicit subsidies.) Some states provide additional explicit subsidies.

An additional hidden subsidy is made possible by the special, five-year, accounting depreciation that applies to wind or solar. A natural gas plant, in contrast, must be depreciated over 20-years. By quickly depreciating the capital cost, a highly taxed corporate investor can get a rapid tax deduction, essentially paying for a leveraged investment in the project in 5 years or less by reducing federal and state income tax. Because the investment is leveraged with debt, the investor expects to recover more than his original investment. This is called tax equity financing. A better description is tax loophole financing, making it possible for profitable companies to increase their profits by financing renewable energy projects at the expense of the government. (Due to the new Trump tax law a change in the economics of tax equity financing is expected, probably making it less attractive due to the lower corporate tax rate.)

A subtler hidden subsidy is the favorable policy treatment given to wind and solar. For example, a guaranteed long term market at a fixed price, or generous regulatory treatment.

The explicit and hidden subsidies are giveaways to special interests. The special interests wrap themselves in a green flag to justify why they should receive billions from the state and federal treasuries.

The financing of renewable energy can be massively complicated, involving hundreds of thousands of dollars of legal fees. The lawyer's job is to make the project seem to be a regular business rather than a tax dodge. The complicated nature of the financing helps hide the true economic situation from the public.

The Lazard company is a financial advisory firm that has renewable energy clients. Lazard publishes a popular annual estimate of the cost of various types of renewable energy. The company claims not to include subsidies in its analysis, but leaves in the tax equity subsidy, as if it isn't a subsidy. By not treating tax equity financing as a subsidy, Lazard makes wind energy seem cheaper than it really is. Lazard also explicitly states that it doesn't account for the costs imposed by the erratic nature of renewable energy – a very important cost. They compare costs at the plant fence, a faulty method of comparison as explained previously. In this manner, without actually telling lies, its analysts promote the idea that renewable energy is competitive with traditional energy even if there were no subsidies.

Calculating the cost of electricity is not an exact science. Future trends are guesses. For example, estimating the cost of natural gas 25 years in the future is very speculative as both supply and demand are subject to economic trends and technology changes, not just in the U.S., but worldwide. The siting of power plants depends on such things as powerline paths, the location of natural gas lines, water ways, and railroads. Advocates of wind are likely to argue that the capital cost of wind power is declining. But so is the cost of natural gas plants. The National Renewable Energy Laboratory estimated the cost of combined cycle natural gas plants at $1359 (2015 dollars) per kW of nameplate capacity, in 2012. By 2017 this was reduced to $1032 (2015 dollars), a real decline of 24% in 5 years. Natural gas fuel has also declined in price. It may be that the cost of natural gas will increase in the future as gas exports increase. But it is also possible that increasing production of natural gas will lower the price.

The discount rate or interest rate used when calculating the cost of electricity affects the contribution of capital investment to the cost per kWh of electricity. The discount rate is the index used to discount the value of money received in the future and is closely related to the interest rate. A low discount rate makes wind and solar more valuable, because the future revenues are more valuable compared to the immediate capital cost. For fossil fuel generation, the discount rate has less effect because fuel is a big expense not affected by the discount rate. Thus, the proponents of wind or solar can be expected to argue for a low discount rate or interest rate, to make their energy pencil out cheaper.

The 8 percent discount and interest rate I use is consistent with the rate used by various authorities. For example, the Lazard company uses 8 percent as the interest rate for money borrowed to finance renewable energy projects. The Energy Information Administration uses 7.5 percent.[10] Eight percent is actually a low interest rate if renewable energy projects stood on their own. But most projects have long term contracts with a utility that effectively is backed by the government, since electricity supply must be preserved at all costs. Although utilities have gone bankrupt, they keep operating. In the current political environment, in my opinion, it is not likely that power purchase contracts with renewable energy companies would be canceled in bankruptcy. Neither is it likely that many utilities will go bankrupt. According to Lazard, the equity investors, putting up front money, typically require 12 percent return, as they assume the most risk.

Some advocates of capital investment to prevent distant and hypothetical global warming, have argued for very low discount

---

[10] The Electricity Market Module of the National Energy Modeling System: Model Documentation 2014

rates, in the region of 1 percent. For example, the *Stern Review* on the economics of climate change, a report commissioned by the British Government, advocated very low discount rates. In this way analysts, can justify financing projects that will supposedly payoff in 100 years by preventing the hypothetical global warming. Without a low discount rate, what happens in 100 years is irrelevant to the current economy and no project that has its payoff 100 years in the future can be justified. With an 8% discount rate, $1000 dollars received in 100 years is valued at 45 cents today. But if the discount rate is 1% then $1000 in 100 year is valued at $369 today.

The Carbon Reduction Fallacy

A global warming believer might say, yes, we waste 5 cents for every kWh hour generated by wind or solar, but that is solely economic. The wasted money, or subsidy, is the price we pay to reduce the amount of CO_2 emitted. The global warming believers claim all sorts of fantastic disasters from CO_2 emissions, so any cost can easily be justified for reducing CO_2. The money is being spent now for a future, highly dubious, and highly discounted event. My opinion is that the well–known benefits of CO_2 for agriculture, making plants grow better and with less water, outweigh any benefit from reducing CO_2 emissions. Thus, there is every reason to welcome CO_2 emissions. [Yes, this goes against conventional wisdom and years of propaganda.] CO_2 emissions are aerial fertilizer. It is possible to calculate the cost of using wind or solar to reduce CO_2 emissions in comparison to other methods of reducing CO_2 emissions.

Wind is subsidized by about 5.1 cents per kWh and solar by about 5.6 cents per kWh. That is the difference between the cost and the benefit of fuel saved. If you allocate the subsidy to the task of reducing CO_2 emissions, it can be calculated[11] that it costs around $140 per metric ton of CO_2 emissions avoided by using wind or solar. Avoiding or compensating for a metric ton of CO_2 emissions is known as a carbon offset. Carbon offsets

---

[11] A 117 pounds of CO_2 emissions for each MMBtu of gas according to the EIA. 2.2 cents worth of gas is displaced for each kWh generated or (2.2/320)*117 = .805 lb/kWh. To reduce CO_2 emissions by metric ton requires generating (2204/.804) =2741 kWh. The subsidy cost if .051*2741 = $139 per tonne for wind and .056*2741 = $153 per tonne for solar.

are traded, and a carbon offset can be purchased from, for example, carbonfund.org for $10 for a metric ton of CO_2 reduction. That organization has various methods of compensating for CO_2 emissions, such as planting trees. Wind and solar are hopelessly expensive methods for avoiding CO_2 emissions.

Propaganda and Greenspeaking

This chapter reviews the propaganda that has enabled the renewable energy industry to obtain a positive public image that it does not deserve.

The renewable energy industry has excellent public relations. Much press coverage is fawning and massively ignorant. For example, the New York Times ran a February 6, 2018 op-ed: *Why a Big Utility Is embracing Wind and Solar.* The article claims that wind and solar are replacing coal powered plants. But wind and solar don't replace anything because the conventional grid has to be in place as backup to the erratic output of wind and solar. If coal plants are closed, they are typically replaced by natural gas plants, not wind and solar. The article claims that power bills in Colorado will fall as a result of building more wind and solar. That is unlikely, even with the generous federal subsidies for wind and solar. In any case the subsidies simply remove money from your electric bill and add it to your tax bill. The article implies that the cost of batteries will decline, and batteries will help to manage the erratic output of wind and solar plants. That argument has been dispatched in the previous chapter.

Edward Bernays is considered the father of modern public relations. He wrote a seminal book, *Propaganda*, published in 1928. He pointed out that men's ideas and beliefs are largely determined by propaganda, or ideas and opinions presented from authoritative sources. In 1928 the word propaganda was not as sinister as it is now.

The institutions and leaders that disseminate renewable energy propaganda are themselves influenced by smaller groups with more strongly held ideas and opinions. Not every op-ed writer or broadcaster is a fanatic supporter of renewable energy. Like the public, they are influenced by others, individuals more intensely committed to renewable energy. Those who are strongly committed, are either ideologically committed to the idea of renewable energy, or have something to sell. The people and organizations that are strong supporters of renewable energy actively propagandize the general public and especially the opinion leaders in media, academia and politics who are in a position to amplify the message.

Several years ago, I was speaking to a congressman at a fund raiser. I was explaining the case against wind energy and the case against the federal subsidies for wind energy. Another man was quietly listening. After I finished my spiel, I was introduced to the other man who turned out to be a lobbyist for wind energy and a longtime supporter of the congressman. The lesson for me was that it is hard to compete with paid propagandists.

The lies and exaggerations in support of renewable energy are many. The most important lies are that renewable energy is competitive with fossil fuels and that it will effectively aid in preventing a global warming catastrophe.

In practice, renewable energy is wind and solar electricity. Other types of renewable energy – for example, methane gas from rotting material in garbage dumps – are niche players. The promoters of wind and solar electricity claim many advantages. Most of those advantages are non-existent. On the other hand, these promoters demonize their main competitor, fossil fuel generating plants.

The Union of Concerned Scientists[12] claims that renewable energy is vast and inexhaustible, it will provide stable energy prices, and it will produce jobs and other economic benefits. They say that fossil fuel plants are linked to "breathing problems, neurological damage, heart attacks, and cancer." Scaring people with the word "cancer" is ever popular.

The Sierra Club has a discussion of coal plants aimed at 5th graders:

> It's time to act now to stop carbon pollution. Carbon pollution is the main contributor to climate disruption, making extreme weather worse – including more severe floods, widespread wildfires and record drought. It is also linked to life-threatening air pollution— such as the smog that can trigger asthma attacks.[13]

Notice that "global warming" has been replaced with "climate disruption" and "extreme weather." Global warming has been largely retired due to lack of warming (see chapter 3). The notion that global warming will create floods, droughts and wildfires is simply propaganda without serious scientific backing.

Greenspeaking

Propagandists, as George Orwell noticed, tamper with the language. In Orwell's novel, *1984*, the tyrannical government promotes a constricted language called Newspeak. Newspeak was designed to limit freedom of thought by removing certain words from the language and changing the meaning of other words. The propagandists for renewable power are practicing their own version of Newspeak: let's call it greenspeak. The greenspeakers have tampered with the meaning of the word pollution. Pollution of the air formerly meant adding toxic or poisonous substances to the air. But now, carbon dioxide has become pollution, even though is a colorless, odorless gas. It is

---

[12] Union of Concerned Scientists: Benefits of Renewable Energy Use -on website ucsusa.org

[13] https://content.sierraclub.org/coal/burning-carbon-pollution-and-climate-disruption

not toxic to animals or people and it is an essential nutrient for plant life. Now, however, the propagandists incessantly refer to "carbon pollution." Whatever effect carbon dioxide may have on climate; it is not air pollution.

The greenspeakers are engaged in a never-ending revision of their vocabulary. According to the satellite measurements of the Earth's temperature, warming has been weak in recent decades. Faced with this catastrophe for their theory, the greenspeakers substituted "climate change" for "global warming." Climate change is vague enough to permit any unusual weather event to be blamed on CO_2.

It is understandable that the general public can be fooled by a propaganda campaign. But, are the experts at public utility commissions, federal agencies and electric utilities fooled? I think the answer is no, at least for the smarter experts. But, the renewable energy fraud has been structured so that these experts believe it to be in their interest to assist the fraud, or at least to keep silent. If the political bosses are supporting renewable energy, it is difficult for government employees, or the recipients of research contracts, to announce that the politicians are wrong. The politicians are responding to political pressure from the industry and environmental groups. In the era of closely contested elections small groups of true believers have disproportionate influence. Global warming is a very important issue for a small group of true believer voters. Global warming, or now climate change, is a political correctness issue for many politicians.

Definition of Renewable Energy

There isn't a logical rationale behind the concept of renewable energy, or even a commonly accepted definition. Rather, renewable energy is the codification of a collection of prejudices.

Wikipedia defines renewable energy as:

> *Renewable energy* is *energy* that is collected from *renewable* resources, which are naturally replenished on a human

timescale, such as sunlight, wind, rain, tides, waves, and geothermal heat.

What is the justification for favoring renewable energy? Renewable Energy World, an online website, gives these justifications:

Clean, environmental benefits.

Will not run out for later generations.

Avoid importing energy and greater energy security from domestic sources.

According to Renewable Energy World's criteria, coal and nuclear should be renewable energy. They are clean, won't run out in any time worth worrying about. There are domestic. U.S. reserves of coal and nuclear fuel good for 500 years.[14] Both fuels are extremely clean, when properly used. But influential green ideologues dislike coal and nuclear. They make sure that those sources of electricity are excluded from lists of officially approved renewable energies.

Columbus discovered America about 500 years ago. We have no idea what the world will be like in another 500 years. It's ridiculous to worry that we will run out of coal in 500 years.

Sometimes, lack of carbon emissions is touted as an advantage of renewable energy. Coal emits plenty of CO_2. Nuclear emits no CO_2 but is still on the green blacklist.

---

[14] Sometimes it is stated that the reserves of uranium are only sufficient for 90 years or some similar figure. However, this is a naive understanding of mineral reserves. Demand drives supply as proven by many case studies and the potential supply of uranium will expand under the forces of demand. In addition, breeder reactors could expand the supply 50 times by converting U238 to U235. Also, thorium is 3 times as common as uranium and could power reactors. The World Nuclear Association has a paper on this subject: *Supply of Uranium – http://www.world-nuclear.org/information-library/nuclear-fuel-cycle/uranium-resources/supply-of-uranium.aspx*

California has law and regulation defining what is and isn't renewable energy.[15] California's definition of renewable energy is not coherent, but codifies green prejudices as practiced in California. Since California is considered a deep green leader among states, what California says carries weight. According to California, wind and solar are renewable. A number of other niche technologies are also renewable, but none of those minor renewable technologies has potential to play more than a small part in any state's energy portfolio. California seemingly doesn't care that some of its officially renewable technologies, such as geothermal heat and garbage dump methane, aren't naturally replenished on a human timescale as required by the Wikipedia definition of renewable energy. Many geothermal wells run out of steam because the hot rocks generating steam eventually cool. Garbage dumps generating methane are renewed, but not naturally, unless garbage trucks are considered natural. California has a blacklist of energies that logically should be renewable but that are politically incorrect for one reason or another.

The strangest item on the California energy blacklist is large hydroelectric plants. Only impracticable, small plants that don't disturb rivers are allowed. Large scale hydro supplies 7 percent of U.S. electricity and clearly meets every definition of renewable. Hydroelectricity is powered by rainfall and is replenished every time it rains. It emits no CO_2. Unlike wind and solar, hydroelectricity is practical. Obviously, the green ideologues are afraid that if they allowed hydroelectricity to be included as renewable, more dams and less wind and solar would be built. The problem seems to be that environmentalists don't like dams. If CO_2-free electricity is so important, why block hydroelectricity just because certain green circles don't like dams?

---

[15] Renewables Portfolio Standard Eligibility, Ninth Edition Revised. California Energy Commission.

Environmental Campaigns Against the Common Good

Environmentalists have been virulently opposed to nuclear energy since the 1970's.[16] They used scare tactics (cancer) similar to the tactics they are using against coal today. The Kyoto protocol was an international agreement designed to limit emissions of carbon dioxide. It included a carbon credit scheme that would enable developers of carbon free energy to receive cash payments. Logically nuclear energy should have been eligible for such payments because nuclear energy is carbon free. But nuclear was explicitly excluded from Kyoto at the behest of environmental lobbyists. They would have been embarrassed if people started building nuclear plants to solve the alleged global warming crisis. There was no logical reason to exclude nuclear given that it is CO_2 free and a practical source of electricity. Yes, nuclear plants can malfunction and kill people, but so can dams and many other types of industrial installations. Very few people have been killed by the hundreds of nuclear plants. France gets 80 percent of its electricity from nuclear and has never had a major accident involving nuclear power. The Japanese Fukushima nuclear plant disaster pointed up weaknesses in some nuclear plants involving emergency cooling and spent fuel pools. One hopes that these weaknesses will be fixed world-wide. Although at Fukushima several reactors were destroyed by meltdown and chemical hydrogen explosions, there was no large release of radiation.

The many causes espoused by the environmental organizations have one thing in common. They alarm the public and get attention, thereby raising money for the environmental organizations. It doesn't matter if the science behind the cause is junk science, as long as it is scary. A tragic example is that environmental organizations succeeded in banning DDT, a uniquely effective (and low toxicity) insecticide for suppressing malaria mosquitos. As a result, several million children in Africa died from malaria while DDT was banned in most countries. Thankfully, the World Health Organization came out in favor of resuming the use of DDT. Nobody is holding the environmental

---

[16] The Death and Possible Revival of nuclear Power in The USA. Poster American Geophysical Union Science Policy Conference, June 2013, Washington, DC. http://www.climateviews.com/uploads/6/0/1/0/60100361/posteragu-spf-pdf-reduced.pdf

Propaganda and Greenspeaking

organizations accountable for the deaths of millions of African children. The environmental organizations seemingly enjoy special immunities. They consistently do things that others can't, not just killing African children, but such things as filing frivolous lawsuits, or telling us that everything they don't like causes cancer.

The Sierra Club has a campaign[17] to get cities to pledge to use 100 percent renewable energy by a date in the future. According to the Sierra Club 150 mayors have endorsed the idea that their cities should run on 100 percent renewable power. This campaign is obviously intended to convince people that running on 100 percent renewable energy is a feasible idea. The campaign is deceptive. An endorsement by a mayor is not the same as a law passed by the city government, and especially nothing like having an actual plan to make this happen. A mayor's endorsement is simply a publicity gimmick. And, in any event, most cities have little or no control over their electrical system or where the power comes from. That authority usually resides with public utility commissions and state and federal governments.

All sources of electricity are mixed together in the electrical grid. So, when a city draws power from the grid, it is getting only a small proportion of renewable power, around 7 percent on average. How can a city set a goal of 100 percent renewable power and become a member of the Sierra Club's group of 100 percent cities?

One could try to track the flow of electricity in the grid in order to allocate power drawn by a city from different generating facilities. The trivial result would be that more power comes from nearby generating plants than from distant plants. It is not technically feasible to route a particular source of power from one place to another on the grid.

To meet impossible renewable energy pledges, cities, states and corporations use an accounting trick called a Renewable Energy Certificate or a REC. Producers of renewable power sell the certificates. The certificates are considered to give the

---

[17] https://www.sierraclub.org/ready-for-100

purchasers the right to claim that they are using renewable power, even though the actual renewable power is used someplace else. Each certificate represents one megawatt hour of renewable electricity. Buying a certificate allows the purchaser of the certificate to claim to be using renewable electricity even though it isn't. Thus, a city or company can claim to use 100 percent renewable power if it buys enough certificates. But the city or company is actually using whatever power comes out of the grid where it is located. RECs are an officially sanctioned scheme for misleading to the public. RECs also provide an additional source of subsidy for renewable power.

An argument can be made that RECs are justified as a device to promote the development of renewable power. But it is not honest to give the public the impression that the purchaser of RECs is actually using renewable power.

The propagandists for wind and solar use fake photography to give the impression that smokestacks of conventional fossil fuel plants are belching toxic black smoke. This outright fakery says a lot about the ethics of the Sierra Club and similar organizations. The picture is an example that appeared on the

Sierra Club website.[18] The smokestack is actually belching harmless water vapor. When the water vapor or steam hits the cool air, it condenses into a white cloud. By photographing with the sun behind the smoke stack, the white cloud of water droplets can be made to appear black. It is revealing that, in the photo, there is no "smoke" immediately above the stack before the water vapor has mixed with the cool air sufficiently to condense. Depending on the temperature and humidity, the water vapor may not condense at all. In that case, nothing seems to be coming out of a stack.

The next picture is a modern coal plant, the John W. Turk Jr. plant, in Arkansas. It was operating at full power when this photo was taken. Nothing is visible exiting the smokestack. But water vapor and carbon dioxide, the products of combustion, are coming out of the stack. Pollutants have been reduced to low levels by various pollution scrubbers.

John W. Turk Coal Plant at Full Power

---

[18] https://www.sierraclub.org/sierra/can-trump-really-repeal-clean-power-plan

The next picture is a Tampa Electric, 1700 megawatt coal powered generating complex, operated by Tampa Electric near Apollo Beach, Florida. The condensing steam rapidly evaporates after it exits the stack. The body of water is used to supply cooling water for the plant, and as a result it is warmed above the temperature of the adjacent ocean. Sea life is drawn to shelter in the warm water during the Florida winter. The small objects in the water are the heads of mantees, aquatic plant eating mammals.

The Sierra Club claims that coal power plants cause asthma attacks, an idea not supported by science. Pollution from modern coal plants is very low and, in any case, medical science does not know the cause of asthma, although it is suspected it is encouraged by excessively clean environments experienced by children in advanced countries, which do not condition children's immune systems for allergens. Children in homes with dogs experience less asthma. Asthma is rare in backward countries where children live in contaminated environments. Bizarrely, coal plants might prevent asthma if only they actually were dirty.

Green Ideologues

The picture that emerges from examining the tactics and history of the green ideologues is that they adopt policies and tactics that make good propaganda rather than good science. Inconsistencies are papered over or hidden. The greens seek money or power under the guise of doing good. The various green organizations are financially very successful. For example, the Sierra Club has annual revenues over $100 million.

The advocates of wind and solar depict themselves as noble fighters against evil forces. The evil forces are usually fossil fuel companies. The problem with that story is that those companies actually take the side of the promoters of wind and solar. The companies are too timid, or too smart, to take on the politically powerful green forces.

If you consult the Chevron or ExxonMobil websites, you will discover that these giant companies are researching and investing in renewable energy. For example, ExxonMobil says that it is "partnering with leading universities to develop new energy technologies, improve energy efficiency and reduce greenhouse gas emissions." Fossil fuel companies have made large financial contributions to various green organizations. These are best viewed as protection payments. However ideological crusaders don't stay bought for very long. The natural gas industry gave the Sierra Club $25 million only to have the Sierra Club viciously attack fracking with a storm of lies and exaggerations.

There are many scientists and economists that reject green ideology and reject the ideology's inconsistent and wrong ideas about reforming the economy. There are a number of non-profit think tanks that question the utility of wind and solar. Think tanks like the Institute for Energy Research or the Heartland Institute have tiny budgets in comparison to the environmental organizations. These fighters against the green giant get almost no money from coal or oil related interests.

Citizens that oppose green ideology are subjected to campaigns of intimidation, even including lengthy and expensive lawsuits. A Stanford University professor, Mark Z. Jacobson and coauthors, wrote a paper proposing that the U.S. could operate 100 percent on renewable energy by 2055. His paper gives some detail as to how this could supposedly be done. Another scientist, Christopher T.M. Clack and coauthors, wrote a paper disputing Jacobson's paper. Jacobson then sued Clack and the Clack's publisher for $10 million. Lawsuits are not a normal method of settling scientific disputes. But lawsuits are good for shutting up people that utter politically incorrect ideas.

In my opinion (don't sue me), Jacobson's idea of 100 percent renewable energy by 2055, besides being impracticable, is also silly. There is no good reason to go to 100 percent renewable energy. If you believe in global warming the answer is nuclear. If you're worried about running out of fuel the answer is coal, natural gas, or nuclear. None of these is officially renewable. But if you're a believer in renewable, the answer is wind, solar, and hydrogen. Jacobson proposes a new generation of fat airplanes running on liquid hydrogen. Unfortunately, the fuel tanks have to be four times larger to hold the same amount of energy as in jet fuel. The fuel tanks would also have to be well insulated since liquid hydrogen boils at the incredibly cold temperature of minus 423 degrees Fahrenheit.

A characteristic of green ideology is selective technological optimism. A favorite technique for estimating future costs is to extrapolate recent trends. The cost of new technologies declines in the early stages, but often the rate of improvement bottoms out after economies of scale and economies of experience are exhausted. For wind energy, the bottom seems to have been reached. The National Renewable Energy Laboratory commissioned a study: *Cost and Performance Data for Power Generation Technologies* and an update to the report: *NREL Costs 2017-ATB-data*. That report estimates the capital cost (in constant 2015 dollars) of onshore wind at $1542 per kW in 2018, which will decline to $1419 by 2028. For photovoltaic solar, they project a cost decline from $1148 per kW to $947 by 2028. Over 10-years they predict an 8% cost decline for wind and 18% for solar. Keep in mind that the National *Renewable Energy* Laboratory is unlikely to have a negative view of the future of wind and solar. The Chinese are also drastically cutting subsidies for selling solar panels at a loss. That may drive up the cost of solar.

Another factor for both solar and wind is the using up of the best locations. A good location is near a power line with spare capacity, with available land and with good wind or sun.

Wind Turbine Blade Iowa

The greenies get very excited about the past declines in the cost of wind turbines and solar panels. But they probably don't mention that the cost of natural gas generating plants, as well as the cost of the natural gas fuel, is also dropping rapidly.

Wind turbines are constructed mostly from concrete and steel. The very large components are moved to remote locations with difficulty. In order to make wind turbines cheaper, one path is to make them larger. The power that can be generated is proportional to the swept area of the rotor. Doubling the height of the turbine would make the swept area 4 times larger for the same proportions. The assumption is that a very large turbine is cheaper than 2 or 3 smaller turbines. Very large turbines are most practical for offshore wind farms. It is easier to transport large components over water than over land. But, offshore wind farms are very expensive for a variety of reasons. The largest turbines currently available are in the 5-10 megawatt class and may approach 50 stories in height. In order to transport and install them over land, the components have to be assembled from manageable-sized parts. This could be done. After all, the construction of skyscrapers is routine. But it seems likely, as the National Renewable Energy Laboratory projects, that reductions in cost will be moderate. The big problems are still the erratic nature of the power and the limited number of places, often remote, that have good wind.

Which is Dumber, California or Germany?

I have to give the trophy to Germany. It hurts my national pride, given that we Americans like to be first in everything. The Germans beat out Hollywood, San Francisco, and governor Jerry "moonbeam" Brown, by a mile.

Both Germany and California have vast solar power installations, but California is actually sunny. According to Wikipedia, "Germany has about the same solar potential as Alaska, which has an average of 3.08 sun hours/day in Fairbanks." The state of Bavaria has the most solar power in Germany. At the capital of the state, Munich, January solar irradiance is 1.88 kilowatt hours per square meter per day (kWh/m^2/day). In July, the best month, it gets up to 4.68 kWh/m^2/day. In Bakersfield, CA the January irradiance is 2.61 kWh/m^2/day and the July number is 7.71 kWh/m^2/day. Bakersfield has 38 percent more sun in winter and 64 percent more in summer. There are even more sunny places in California, for example, Death Valley and similar desert areas, where the sun shines incessantly.

Electricity in Germany costs an average of 37 cents per kWh. In California, in spite of trying hard to screw things up, it is only 15 cents, much more than most states of the U.S., but a bargain compared to Germany. In neighboring France, electricity is about 18 cents per kWh, including substantial taxes. France is heavily nuclear.

Germany has spent lavishly on solar and wind in its quest to reduce CO_2 emissions to prevent global warming. But due to fear of nuclear power the Germans are closing nuclear plants. As a consequence, they have had to greatly increase the use of coal, the greatest emitter of CO_2 among the fossil fuels.

There may be a connection between the fact that Germany is a pleasant and prosperous country and the fact that it has a strident and unrealistic green movement. Not having real problems, it may be necessary to invent problems. The website *No Tricks Zone* keeps English speakers abreast of the craziness that is German energy.

More Thoughts and Problems

Wind and solar energy come in many versions and create many problems. This chapter collects some of those problems and speculates about the future.

The Future of Existing Wind and Solar Installations

Once wind or solar installations have been built, the capital cost becomes sunk investment. If policy could be changed, so that we are no longer required to purchase over-priced power, foisted on the public by global warming scare stories, most wind or solar plants would be forced into bankruptcy. The decision to continue operating the facilities would be independent of how much money was spent to construct them. Most facilities have long term power delivery contracts, but even those contracts can, at least in theory, be abrogated by bankruptcy. The operating cost of wind farms is quite high, working out to about 1.6 cents per kWh. Solar farms have lower operating costs. In both cases the operating cost is less than the 2.2 cents of fuel saving generated by operating the plants. Those numbers, from the viewpoint of cash flow, suggest that the existing plants, one they shed their debts in bankruptcy, should be retained since they seem economically viable, by a narrow margin. But the symbolism would be better if they are torn down to kill the renewable energy myth once and for all. Bird lovers would appreciate and end to windmills chopping up birds.

The Residential Rooftop Solar Scam

The sales pitch for residential rooftop solar is that it will reduce your electric bill and you can sell the excess energy that you don't consume back to the electric company. Rooftop solar may be profitable for the homeowner, depending on how much electricity costs, depending on how much the power company will pay you for power you feed back into the grid, and depending on how big the various subsidies are. The capital cost of rooftop residential solar is more than three times higher than large scale utility solar per kW of capacity. The electricity generated often costs 30 cents per kWh without subsidies.

As part of an economically rational structure, be assured that rooftop solar is not remotely competitive. It is a complete waste of money. But public policy concerning solar electricity is not rational, so it can be a good choice for certain homeowners if the current electric rate structures and subsidies continue for the next 20 years or so.

Rooftop solar is eligible for a 30 percent capital investment subsidy from the federal government. Additional subsidies are sometimes available. The higher the cost of electricity, the more attractive rooftop solar is. California has a policy of charging exorbitant electric rates for private homes that consume larger amounts of electricity, so rooftop solar is popular in California.

The *Wall Street Journal* in an April 17, 2017 opinion article, *Thanks for Giving Me Your Tax Money,* recounts the experience of an Austin, Texas homeowner. He installed a rooftop solar system that exclusive of subsidies cost about $32,000. He received about $14,000 in subsidies. His system has a nameplate capacity of 8.5 kW. Assuming a capacity factor of 16 percent, a reasonable figure for a rooftop system in a reasonably sunny area, the system will generate 12,000 kWh per year. If the $32,000 cost were financed at 8 percent for 20 years, the annual payment would be $3,259. The cost of the electricity works out to 27 cents per kWh without subsidies. If you include the $14,000 worth of subsidies, then the cost works out to 15 cents per kWh. If the interest rate was 4 percent instead of 8 percent, possible if the person's house is used as security for the loan, the cost with subsidies becomes 11 cents per kWh. (These numbers ignore ongoing maintenance.)

In the example above the cost of rooftop solar varies from 27 cents per kWh to 11 cents per kWh depending on subsidies and interest rates. Whether solar is cost-effective depends on how the utility's relationship with rooftop solar is structured. Solar is profitable in jurisdictions where electric rates are exorbitant and/or the payment for electricity fed back into the grid is generous. California is the champion of high electric rates; the state has a tiered system where larger consumers pay more than 50 cents per kWh. The city of Austin, Texas, also has a tiered system, but the allowances and rates are far more helpful to rooftop solar economics in California, since California's rates are more punitive against the users of conventional electricity.

Charging 50 cents per kWh for electricity is outrageous. The wholesale cost of electricity (not renewable, of course) is usually less than 6 cents per kWh. But the homeowner who cuts his bill in half by installing solar may not realize that he is achieving his savings at the expense of taxpayers and other electricity consumers. He may even think that rooftop solar electricity is cheaper than fossil fuel electricity. It is for him – because everyone else is paying for it.

The only economic benefit of rooftop solar is saving about two cents per kWh for fuel saved in backup natural gas plants. If the rooftop solar, without subsidies, costs 30 cents per kWh then the subsidy is 30 cents minus two cents or 28 cents per kWh. Given these numbers rooftop solar is 93% subsidized. The subsidy comes from explicit subsidies, payment for power fed back into the grid and lost utility revenue that must be made up by higher rates. If the homeowner makes a profit compared to not having rooftop solar, then the subsidy is even higher. If the subsidy is justified on global warming grounds and the subsidy is considered a payment for a carbon offset, then carbon offsets for a metric ton of CO_2 are being purchased for $800 each.[19] Such offsets can be purchased in the carbon offset market for about $10.

The Duck Curve and California Solar

Solar electricity peaks during the day and drops rapidly as sunset nears. But peak demand for electricity usually ramps up just as the solar electricity is fading away. The duck curve shows the generation by the rest of the grid, other than solar. A typical example from California is below. The name duck curve comes from the resemblance of the curve to the back of a duck. Due to the large amount of solar during midday, the backup gas turbines have to be throttled back while solar generation is strong. The rest of the grid can only be throttled back so far for various reasons, economic and technical. When the limit is reached, solar must be curtailed. As the solar fades at sunset the rest of the grid has to ramp up very quickly. The fast ramp is a difficult trick that stresses the agility of the backup generation.

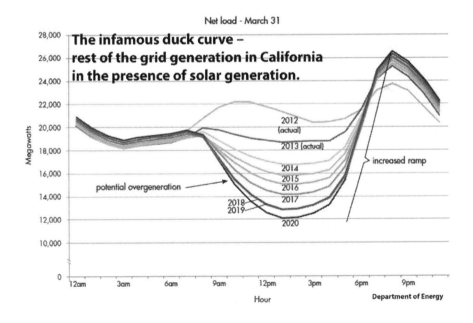

Net load - March 31

The infamous duck curve – rest of the grid generation in California in the presence of solar generation.

---

[19] A gas plant at 50% efficiency releases .34 kg of CO2 per kWh. 2900 kWh generated releases 1000 kg. Applying the 28 cents per kWh subsidy toward the carbon offset the cost of the carbon offset is $0.28*2900 or about $800.

The duck curve situation is worst in the spring when sunshine is plentiful but large, daytime air conditioning loads have not kicked in yet. The duck curve shows that there is a limit to how much solar can be developed without modifying the rest of the grid. One proposed solution is to store solar electricity during the day and release the stored electricity in the early evening. The problem is that storage of electricity is too expensive.

The Cost of Batteries for Electricity Storage

There is much hype about batteries. It is suggested that the price of batteries is dropping and that batteries can be used to smooth the erratic power delivery from wind and solar. Batteries are extremely expensive for storing electricity. Using lithium ion batteries to shift solar power from midday to early evening increases the cost of utility scale solar power from approximately 7.5 cents per kWh to 18.5 cents per kWh. Under this scenario, power that is already not remotely competitive becomes exorbitantly expensive. A simple analysis below shows this.

The Tesla *Power Wall* lithium ion battery costs $3000 and stores 7 kWh of electricity. The Power Wall is not a utility scale battery, so we cut the price in half to $1500 to estimate the cost of utility scale batteries. That makes for an estimate for the price of battery storage as $1500/7= $214 per kWh.

McKinsey & Company in an article, *The New Economics of Energy Storage,* estimate the cost of energy storage as $200 per kWh in 2020 and dropping to $160 by 2025.

Taking 1 kWh of capacity, assume the battery is used reduce daytime solar peaks for 8-hours each day and then release the stored energy for 8-hours each evening. For 8-hours at midday, the battery can be charged, and for 8-hours the 1-kWh battery it will deliver electricity, at a rate of 125 watts. The cost per kWh of capacity is $214. If the life of the battery is ten years and the discount rate is 8 percent, the capital cost per year is close to $32 for each kWh of capacity. The battery won't last much longer than 10 years. During the year for each kWh of capacity the battery will deliver 365 kWh. The capital cost per kWh is $32/365= 8.75

cents per kWh. So far that is the cost for a perfect battery with no additional equipment such as inverters to change DC to AC and vice versa. The battery is rated as 92 percent efficient. If we add 15% to allow for losses in the battery and inverter as well as another 10% for the cost of the inverters and controls, and 7.55 cents per kWh for the solar input power, then 8.75 cents becomes 18.5 cents per kWh. [7.55+1.25*8.75] Peaks can be shaved using gas turbines operating at 16% capacity factor for around 10 cents per kWh. (The low capacity factor greatly increases the cost of the electricity from the gas turbine.)

Adding wind and solar to the power grid creates numerous problems. Battery storage may have a role to aid in increasing grid agility. It might find a role as fast responding reserve power, supplying power for 10 minutes while gas turbines are fired up. In that role, the configuration would be different, supplying a burst of power for 10-minutes instead of supplementary power for 4-hours as in peak shaving. A gas turbine has the advantage that there is not a limit of how long it can supply power. Gas turbines last for decades with daily cycling. Batteries wear out after some number of charge-discharge cycles.

Quick start gas turbine power buffering is much easier than smoothing the output of a wind turbine or a solar farm. In order to get a better idea of the size of the battery needed to smooth the output of a large wind installation I estimated the size of battery that would be needed to smooth the output of the Texas 17-thousand megawatt of nameplate capacity wind farms. In 2016 the average output of Texas the wind system was 6045 megawatts, a 35% capacity factor. I ran an hour by hour simulated test where the battery was charged when power generation was above the average and discharged to keep the power at the average when power generation fell below the average. In order to keep the battery from running flat it had to hold 430 hours of average output or 2.6 million megawatt hours. A battery that big would cost about half trillion dollars at $200 per kWh, or about ten to fifteen times what all the wind turbines in Texas cost. The simulated graph of battery charge for the year of 8760 hours in 2016 is shown in the graph below. If only maintaining 4000 megawatts, instead of 6045 megawatts, was set as the goal, then a battery about 1/4th as large could do that. That battery would "only" cost three times what all the wind farms in Texas cost. Clearly battery storage is infeasible, except for very short term storage.

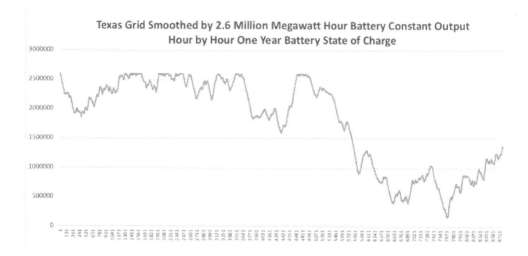

Texas Grid Smoothed by 2.6 Million Megawatt Hour Battery Constant Output Hour by Hour One Year Battery State of Charge

How Subsidies Probably Make an Amazon Solar Roof Profitable

Amazon is an amazing company and a company not given to ostentatious bragging about its green footprint. Amazon is often attacked by green groups for not being green enough. If the federal government and the state of New Jersey insist on granting huge incentives for using solar power, it is hard to fault Amazon for accepting these gifts.

The Amazon company placed a 7.5-megawatt (nameplate) rooftop solar array on top of a 1-million square foot warehouse in Carteret, New Jersey. The solar array is claimed to supply 80% of the energy requirement of the facility. The array generates excess power when solar power production is high, power that is fed into the grid. New Jersey implements net-metering, meaning that Amazon gets credit for electricity fed into the grid at full retail price. The average price for industrial electricity in New Jersey is 10.52 cents per kWh. Unsubsidized, the electricity from the solar array would cost close to 7.5 cents per kWh. Amazon receives a 30% tax credit against the cost of the array and can depreciate the array over 5 years receiving an additional subsidy via reduction in corporate income tax of 30% (21% federal corporate tax an 9% state corporate tax). Approximately half the cost of the array is effectively subsidized by the federal and state governments. These subsidies reduce the cost of the solar electricity to approximately 4 cents per kWh. The capacity factor for solar at the location is approximately 19%. The array will generate about 12,500 MWh per year at a net cost to Amazon of about $40 per MWh. Amazon receives payment or reduction in its electric bill at the rate of $105 per MWh or a cost reduction compared to not having solar of $65 per MWh. The total reduction in the cost of electricity is $812,000 per year. The cost to Amazon for the 20% of energy not covered by solar is about $328,000.

These figures are approximate and speculative since they are based on generic estimates without access to Amazon's detailed accounting. Net metering at full retail price effectively provides a storage mechanism for electricity, even to the extent of storing excess summer production for winter use. There is no actual storage. Utility generation is curtailed to accommodate feed in from Amazon's solar roof. The cost to taxpayers and electricity consumers is substantial.

Fake Science and Global Warming

Global warming – alias extreme weather and alias climate disruption – is a theory of impending catastrophe. Global warming is supposed to be triggered by adding greenhouse gases to the atmosphere. Carbon dioxide, emitted by burning fossil fuels is the most important of these greenhouse gases. A gas that absorbs infrared radiation (heat radiation) is a greenhouse gas. One of the supposed advantages of wind and solar electricity is that they don't emit CO_2. That presupposes that emitting CO_2 is bad. Increasing CO_2 in the atmosphere provides benefits for agriculture and for the health of all lands where plants grow. It is plausible that CO_2 may cause some global warming. But the data suggests that the global warming is hypothetical, minor, and not necessarily bad. The data says that the computer models used to project a catastrophe are not to be trusted. Presenting these computer models as crystal balls for looking at the future is about as credible as using real crystal balls.

The reason why a chapter on global warming is included here is that global warming is one of the major reasons cited for promoting wind and solar energy. Wind and solar are expensive and impracticable devices for reducing CO_2 emissions as shown previously. For that reason, even if you believe the promoters of global warming, it does not logically follow that the right policy is to start installing windmills or solar farms. The right policy would be to start building CO_2-free nuclear and hydro.

Another reason to talk about global warming is that, like renewable energy, global warming is another marcher in the parade of phony impending catastrophes that are the bread and butter of the environmental movement. Exposing the global warming scare lends more credibility to the idea that the public is being played by an alliance of self-interested, environmental, political and scientific pressure groups.

The idea that building windmills and solar farms will save us from global warming suffers from giant logical inconsistencies, even by the frame of reference of the global warming believers. CO_2 emissions are primarily from Asia where they are growing fast. U.S. emissions have been declining due to energy conservation and natural gas displacing coal for electricity generation. By the very theories of the believers in global warming, we are wasting our time trying to reduce U.S. emissions while emissions in Asia dwarf those of the U.S. and are increasing rapidly. There are many ways to decrease CO_2 emissions, building windmills and solar farms are among the most expensive ways.

The science behind global warming is depicted as rock solid by the advocates of global warming. The reality is that the science is slipshod and characterized by constant excuses to explain why the global warming predictions aren't being realized. More sinister is the manipulation and misrepresentation of climate data in order to make it appear that the measured data concerning the Earth's climate better matches the computer predictions of global warming.

The predictions of global warming doom are based on computer models of the Earth's atmosphere. Models from different modeling groups don't agree with each other, by a factor of two or more, concerning the warming effect. Certain model predictions, such as the existence of faster warming at high altitude in the tropics, are not verified, in spite of many excuse-making scientific papers. The only Earth data that exhibits some agreement with the models is the warming after 1975. Prior to 1975 there was not enough CO_2 added to the atmosphere to have a substantial effect, according to the same theories put forth by the proselytizers of global warming. The models cannot explain the strong warming episode from 1910 to 1940 when CO_2 was not an issue. There are alternative theories to explain the changes in the climate of the Earth that have been observed, either historical or recent. The advocates of the CO_2 theory tend to emphasize their theory to the exclusion of other explanations.

The behavior of the advocates of global warming, including scientists and scientific organizations, is characterized by intolerance toward any dissenting opinion and active measures to discredit and marginalize anyone who questions their thesis. They act like a fanatical cult, rather than scientific investigators or open-minded persons listening to evidence.

Prophet of Global Warming: James Hansen

The current global warming scare was largely popularized by one man. James Hansen was the head of a government science laboratory located in Manhattan. Hansen, now retired, is a green ideologue as well as a master publicist. He is shown below at a demonstration opposing coal mining.

Hansen is given to making extreme statements.[20] He compared coal trains to death trains carrying Jews to death camps. He suggested that fossil fuel executives should be put on trial for crimes against humanity. He equated the fight to end climate change to the fight to end slavery.

---

[20] http://leftexposed.org/2015/08/james-hansen/

Hansen's messages are mixed. He wraps himself in moral authority by comparing his cause to protesting the Holocaust and fighting slavery. But he wants to put fossil fuel executives on trial for not submitting to his theories concerning global warming. Actually, most fossil fuel executives, or at least their companies, pay lip service to global warming. Their real crime is that they are members of a collective group that Hansen doesn't like. He has simply invented a new type of Jew, and everyone who does not submit to his theories of global warming, or is a fossil fuel executive, will be sent to prison. His threats should be taken seriously. Fanatics don't respect limits as to how they will treat their opponents. If Hansen says non-believers in global warming, or members of groups he doesn't like, should be put in jail, in my opinion, he means it. If the history of the 20th century has taught us anything, it has taught us that people like Hansen must be kept away from the levers of power.

One has to give Hansen credit for taking his belief in the CO_2 theory of global warming to a logical conclusion. Hansen and a few other advocates of global warming alarmism, like Stewart Brand, the inventor of the Whole Earth Catalog, have come out in favor of nuclear power.[21] That puts Hansen in opposition to

---

[21] See the Guardian: *Nuclear power paves the only viable path forward on climate change.* U.S. edition 3 Dec 2015.

the advocates of wind and solar. Hansen is at least confronting engineering and economic reality. Hansen has faced up to the reality that nuclear is the only practical path to seriously reducing CO_2 emissions from electric generation.

Hansen is a highly successful politician–scientist. While a government employee, as a prominent prophet of global warming, he was able to ignore the bureaucratic hierarchy. He could ignore his government bosses because he had a large and worshipful political following that provided him with a political base that immunized him against being fired or reined in. He received many lucrative prizes; for example, the Blue Planet Prize of $550,000. While a government employee he traveled the world, apparently at others' expense, giving lectures and receiving awards.

Hansen cultivated an image as a humble scientist fighting for truth against uncaring politicians and sinister fossil fuel interests. Hansen is a talented writer and has a better grasp of climate science than most climate scientists. In my opinion, his science papers and lectures are slanted to support his deep belief in an impending global warming catastrophe.

Corporate Cowardice and Hypocrisy

It is ironic that the fossil fuel companies support global warming alarmism and generally kowtow to the idea of limiting CO_2 emissions. Exxon was a "titanium" donor to the American Geophysical Union, an organization dedicated to the global warming ideology. One suspects that titanium is a new category established at the last minute to accommodate Exxon's donation. Usually, titanium is not considered more honorable than platinum.

The fossil fuel industry seems incapable of thinking for itself about global warming, even though it is in the industry's financial interest to question the current orthodoxy. The people that run these companies are apparently dedicated to the idea that appeasement is the way to deal with your enemies. These are companies with bank accounts beyond counting. They employ legions of scientists. They could easily defend themselves. But they are afraid to give even small amounts to think tanks that are skeptical of global warming.

Sign at American Geophysical Union Annual Meeting

Corporate America behaves in a way exactly opposite the Marxist stereotype. Rather than acting like a swashbuckling captain of industry, the average CEO comes across as a timid supporter of the status quo. It stands to reason: Defying the status quo is risky and failure is not a good recipe for getting promoted in big bureaucracies. So, most of the swashbucklers are eliminated early in their careers. Being risk adverse is itself a risk, since nothing big is accomplished without taking risks.

It's hard to see how appeasing the promoters of global warming is in the interest of the stockholders of fossil fuel companies; companies used as punching bags by organizations that think that all fossil fuels should be left in the ground. If the companies took a more aggressive stand the executives would be attacked, but if they are unwilling to take heat in the interests of their stockholders, why are they there? (And why are they paid so much?)

The Royal Society in England, a formerly distinguished scientific fellowship, attacked Exxon in 2006 for providing relatively trivial amounts to organizations skeptical of global warming. Exxon meekly folded and stopped making even trivial donations to skeptics. Thus, the Royal Society succeeded in further suppressing debate concerning global warming dogma.

Apple is surely one of the most hypocritical companies. Greenwashing is a term used by the left to describe companies that fake concern about the environment for public consumption. Apple is a champion greenwasher; assuming a super green pose, while manufacturing nearly everything in China, a country that is as ungreen as a country can be. Al Gore is on the Apple board of directors and may influence Apple's attempts to paint everything it does green. According the Guardian, Apple CEO, Tim Cook: "...doesn't believe there's a tradeoff between the economy and the environment.[22]" – a statement that simply defies the laws of economics. Apple touts its near 100 percent use of renewable energy at its stores and other facilities. Obviously, Apple is faking its use of renewable energy by buying renewable energy certificates, given that the grid is only about 7 percent renewable energy. Apple is also installing solar panels at various locations. Those, as explained in this book, can be paid for by utilizing tax loopholes and subsidies. Apple would be more convincing if they released a profit and loss statement for their solar energy activities.

Apple may adopt a super green pose to deflect attention from the fact that the company is extremely unpatriotic, supporting hundreds of thousands of jobs in China rather than in the United States. There is no reason why Apple products, products susceptible to automated manufacturing, could not be manufactured in the United States.

---

[22] The Guardian 23 September 2014: Apple CEO Time Cook at Climate Week: 'the time for inaction as passed'

Google is more upfront about its for-profit investments in renewable energy. In an article, Rick Needham, Google's director of energy and sustainability said: "We look at projects that will give us attractive returns.[23]" In the same article, concerning the return on green investments:

> "Google uses tax-equity financing, a government incentive that allows it to lower its tax obligations by investing in renewable energy. Solar projects can produce returns of 10 percent to 14 percent annually, with about half the profit tied to incentives, according to Paul Maxwell, director in the energy practice at Navigant Consulting in Folsom, California."

Scientists and Global Warming

The scientists who are on the global warming skeptics side of the argument are unpopular among their fellow scientists because attacks on global warming alarmism threaten the vast funding apparatus that is the reward for frightening everyone. Skeptic scientists are seen as trying to murder the goose that lays golden eggs. In spite of the risk associated with adopting a skeptical stance toward global warming, there are plenty of skeptic scientists. There is a congressional report[24] that archives statements by hundreds of scientists that believe global warming is bad science. Here is what a few of the dissenting scientists say as quoted on the site climatedepot.com:

> *"Hundreds of billion dollars have been wasted with the attempt of imposing a Anthropogenic Global Warming (AGW) theory that is not supported by physical world evidences...AGW has been forcefully imposed by means of a barrage of scare stories and indoctrination that begins in the elementary school textbooks."* — Brazilian Geologist Geraldo Luís Lino, who authored the 2009 book

---

[23] Bloomberg Technology 9 March 2014: Google Reaps Tax Breaks in $1.4 Billion Clean energy Bet.

[24] More Than 1000 International Scientists Dissent Over Man-Made Global Warming Claims -
http://www.cfact.org/pdf/2010_Senate_Minority_Report.pdf

"The Global Warming Fraud: How a Natural Phenomenon Was Converted into a False World Emergency."
"The dysfunctional nature of the climate sciences is nothing short of a scandal. Science is too important for our society to be misused in the way it has been done within the Climate Science Community." The global warming establishment *"has actively suppressed research results presented by researchers that do not comply with the dogma of the IPCC."* — Swedish Climatologist Dr. Hans Jelbring, of the Paleogeophysics & Geodynamics Unit at Stockholm University.

"The whole idea of anthropogenic global warming is completely unfounded. There appears to have been money gained by Michael Mann, Al Gore and UN IPCC's Rajendra Pachauri as a consequence of this deception, so it's fraud." — South African astrophysicist Hilton Ratcliffe, a member of the Astronomical Society of Southern Africa (ASSA) and the Astronomical Society of the Pacific and a Fellow of the British Institute of Physics.

"In essence, the jig is up. The whole thing is a fraud. And even the fraudsters that fudged data are admitting to temperature history that they used to say didn't happen...Perhaps what has doomed the Climategate fraudsters the most was their brazenness in fudging the data" — Dr. Christopher J. Kobus, Associate Professor of Mechanical Engineering at Oakland University, specializes in alternative energy, thermal transport phenomena, two-phase flow and fluid and thermal energy systems.

The distinguished MIT scientist, Richard Lindzen, has written an essay: *Climate Science: Is it Currently Designed to Answer Questions?*[25] The essay, written from the viewpoint of an insider, demolishes the scientific establishment behind the global warming scare.

---

[25] euresis journal Volume 2 Winter 2012:
http://www.climateviews.com/uploads/6/0/1/0/60100361/lindzenclimatescienceanswerquesstionsejv2id9_sm2008_lindzen.pdf

Lindzen points out that science has become highly bureaucratized and highly dependent on the Federal government. This scientific establishment traffics in fear as an incentive to convince the government and the public that more money is needed for science. The fear can be fear of Russians, fear of disease, fear of environmental destruction, etc. Lindzen sees more emphasis in science on computing and computer modeling as opposed to theory. As a result, standards have declined because it is easier to generate (weak) scientific papers with the aid of computers. Although I often criticize abstract theory not supported by data, theories do hold science together. Often computer models don't contribute to theoretical understanding or are used as a substitute for understanding.

Eisenhower's warning in his 1961 farewell address has come true. Science policy has been taken over by dependence on government money. Government agencies parrot the global warming party line. Things may be getting better with the advent of the Trump administration, but it is not clear that the new administration can continue to withstand attacks for not "listening to science." Listening to science means swallowing every lie told by the science lobby in the pursuit of money. Trump understands that science is another lobby in Washington, DC, not a collection of disinterested big thinkers.

It is amazing how scientific lobbies can disguise self-interest behind a wall of self-righteous and pompous claims of scientific objectivity. The National Academy of Sciences is a prime example. Supposedly that organization grants membership to the nation's most distinguished scientists. However, Richard Lindzen, himself a member since he was 37, has pointed out (in the previously mentioned essay) how green activists have infiltrated the organization and created a route to membership on green political credentials rather than scientific achievement. The academy is largely supported by the federal government. But as an independent organization it is immune to sunshine laws that provide windows into what governments are up to.

The Academy published a study: *A National Strategy for Advancing Climate Modeling*. The study was authored by climate modeling scientists who, of course, have a direct interest in further government support for climate modeling. So, the report obviously suffers from severe credibility problems. Climate modeling is an over-financed area of dubious science. There are dozens of scientific research groups spending government money from many countries on redundant climate models. Naturally, the report urges that more money be spent on climate modeling. I found it amusing that the report urges that a cadre of climate model interpreters be established. These people would be an interface between the climate modeling industry and the public. Since the climate models don't agree with each other, or with the climate of the Earth, interpreters, or spin doctors, are obviously needed. It may also be that the most self-important scientists, slurping at the government trough, feel it is beneath them to justify themselves to the taxpayers, so they would rather have professional P.R. people do it. Or, maybe they prefer to delegate lying to the hired help.

Large bureaucracies and lobbying for money have come to dominate science, but there are still scientists committed to science as a search for truth. Woe unto the scientist who publicly opposes the bureaucratic leaders, at his university or research laboratory, on critical issues related to funding. Scientists are employees of universities or research laboratories. Although it is difficult to fire a scientist at a university or a government lab, there are plenty of ways of making their lives hell. Scientific truth is not a defense for interfering with the flow of money from Washington.

Scientists skeptical of global warming mostly come from allied disciplines rather than mainstream climate science. The pressure to conform is greatest against mainstream climate scientists. Still, there are a number of distinguished mainstream climate scientists that argue strongly against global warming alarmism.

A scholar named James Prall compiled a data base of scientists supporting and opposing the global warming narrative. There were 903 supporters and 472 opponents in his data base. These are scientists who expressed public support on one side or the other. Included in the data base was information about the scientists' education, employment, and scholarly production. Although Prall's intention was undoubtedly to show that the supporters of global warming alarmism were better qualified than the opponents, I analyzed that same data to reveal some other aspects of the nature of the opponents and supporters of global warming. I presented a poster analyzing Prall's data from a different viewpoint at the 2010 Fall Meeting American Geophysical Union.[26] One interesting fact is that there were virtually no young scientist opponents of global warming in mainstream climate science. I attributed this to the pressure to conform being greatest in mainstream climate science and to young scientists being most susceptible to that pressure. Most of the mainstream climate scientists that are skeptical of global warming are older, or even retired, and thus better able to retain their employment or livelihood against attacks on their viewpoint. Young scientists are at the mercy of older mentors, and the community in general for their continued employment and advancement. Science is very much a club. Senior scientists control, publication, hiring, the granting of tenure, and promotions. It is easy for dissenters, especially young dissenters, and especially if they threaten funding, to be blacklisted.

The Intergovernmental Panel on Climate Change (IPCC)

The promoters of global warming established a committee under the auspices of the United Nations, the *Intergovernmental Panel on Climate Change*, or the IPCC. That organization periodically releases impressive seeming reports, supporting the global warming theme. The IPCC's scientific credibility was demolished by the author Donna Laframboise in her book: *The Delinquent Teenager Who Was Mistaken for The World's Top Climate Expert*.[27]

Donna Laframboise exposed the IPCC as a politicized organization promoting global warming alarmism with little scientific foundation. Many of the supposed IPCC scientific experts are poorly qualified activists with unconcealed political agendas. It is practically a law of nature that committees of experts, scientists or not, that are appointed to investigate some question, are always biased in favor of established

---

[26] On my website climateviews.com at:
http://www.climateviews.com/uploads/6/0/1/0/60100361/posteragu2010dist.pdf
[27] https://www.amazon.com/Delinquent-Teenager-Mistaken-Worlds-Climate-ebook/dp/B005UEVB8Q/ref=sr_1_1?ie=UTF8&qid=1514723131&sr=8-1&keywords=the+teenager+ipcc

Fake Science and Global Warming

interests. The experts are the establishment. They are unlikely to endanger their own interests by suggesting that a shakeup of the establishment is needed.

To make things worse, many of the IPCC experts are political activists. Laframboise found that many persons involved with the IPCC have backgrounds with green ideology organizations, such as Greenpeace and the World Wildlife Fund. Some of the so called leading scientists turn out to be graduate students or marginal scientists. Many of the "scientists" are appointed for reasons of geographical or gender diversity and have poor qualifications.

Climate science does not have a firm basis for making long term predictions. Some very long-term predictions are possible, such as expecting another ice age in 10,000 or 20,000 years, the ice ages being driven by astronomical cycles. But making firm predictions of the effect on climate of CO_2 is highly speculative. Even the IPCC does not make a firm claim that the computer models on which it relies are able to make solid predictions. The IPCC calls what the public takes as predictions of doom "projections." A projection is simply the output of a computer model given various inputs and including the many approximations internal to the model. The data from measurements of the Earth's climate strongly suggest that the projections made by the models are wrong. The model projections exaggerate the prospects for CO_2-created global warming. Different models give very different projections of warming. The various models don't use the same inputs. The IPCC, with little justification, simply averages these inconsistent projections.[28] The models are unable to explain important features of the 20th century past climate, particularly the early century warming from 1910 to 1940 and the pause in warming starting in 1998.

If the IPCC did not predict a coming catastrophe, the IPCC would not attract the money and attention that it does. It is hardly likely that the U.N. would finance a purely academic study of the

---

[28] Averaging is justified on the grounds that the average fits past history better than individual models. To the extent that the different models are linearly independent this is an expected consequence of basic curve fitting.

Fake Science and Global Warming

climate that produced truthful reports, concluding that there is a lot we don't know about the climate, and in all probability, the climate will continue on much the same track.

A theory of evolution for science theories and organizations applies here. Organizations that make boring, but truthful, scientific claims don't attract attention and funding. Organizations that make wild claims, predicting disaster, get plenty of attention and funding. Guess what type of science organizations die out and which type of organizations gain money and power. Guess which type of organization receives a Nobel Peace Prize.

The organizations that propagate fake science benefit only as long as it is not widely known that the science is fake. The IPCC Working Group 1 report is over 1500 pages long. The famous novel War and Peace is only 1225 pages long. Longer is not evidence that the science is excellent. The sheer volume of the document precludes a precise critique. The failure to be clear and concise obscures the reality that there is very little sound science in the report. The IPCC chapter on the reliability of the climate models meanders around the serious issues and treats the reader to lengthy but vague discussions about the models. It reminds one of a politician that gives a lengthy answer to a simple question as a way of dodging answering the question.

The original idea of creating a computer model of the Earth's atmosphere to predict future climate trends in response to greenhouse gases may have been a plausible approach. Scientists with more experience in computer modeling probably would have expressed doubts due to the complexity of the problem. In any case, billions of dollars were spent creating climate models of extreme complexity. The scale of the computer models is so great that the world's most powerful computers struggle to run the models on a timescale that permits adequate testing and perfection of the programs. For example, computational cells with dimensions of a kilometer, or often more, make it impossible accurately simulate the land profile or the formation of clouds.

When it turned out that the models disagreed with the climate data collected from the Earth, as well as with models from other labs, the reaction was not to put the model idea aside. Instead the experimenters expanded the modeling efforts to try to force the models to work better. Shockingly, there was a strong tendency to reanalyze the Earth data to make it agree with the models. Given that huge organizations spending billions of dollars had been created around models, the rules of bureaucratic survival drove the modeling efforts to be expanded and justified.

When thousands of jobs and billions of dollars are at risk it is nearly impossible for a scientist to say this isn't working and the entire enterprise should be closed down, or at least drastically cut back. It is much easier to pretend that the models are almost working and maybe with ten or twenty more years of work they will work better. Big bureaucratic entities often degrade into giant and useless paper (or bit) pushing exercises that are difficult to kill. That is the current state of climate modeling.

There are some questionable methods of analysis in the IPPC reports that are worth bringing up. For example, the IPCC often discusses warming prior to 1975 in the context of man-caused global warming. However, by the IPCC's own theories, CO_2 and other greenhouse gases prior to 1975 had too low a rate of increase to have significant influence on the climate. In section TSS.2.2.1 of the Working Group 1 report, the increase in temperature since the 19th century is cited repeatedly. Bringing up temperature changes that don't relate to the CO_2 theory of global warming is simply confusing the issue. Another interesting item in section TSS.2.2.1 is mention of the "Medieval Climate Anomaly." Prior to global warming alarmism, this was called the "Medieval Warm Period." Changing the name is a kind of Greenspeak activity. By changing the name of this period, it is hoped that reality will be changed. It was generally accepted that the climate was warmer from about 1000 AD to 1400 AD, probably warmer than it is today. Climate history was rewritten to change what was a world-wide warming into an anomaly affecting only Europe. A world-wide warming, not related to CO_2, was a threat to the CO_2 theory. The site co2science.org has collected evidence that the warming was indeed world-wide.[29] This controversy relates to the hockey stick controversy. The

---

[29] http://co2science.org/subject/g/summaries/globalmwp.php

hockey stick graph was a graph that purported to show a flat temperature for 1000 years until man started emitting a lot of CO_2 and the temperature shot up. That controversy is too complicated to expound more on here, but the critic Ross McKitrick has posted a summary of the controversy.[30]

Rajendra Pachauri – You Can't Make This Up

The IPCC's credibility was further damaged when the longtime head of the organization, the Indian railroad engineer, Rajendra Pachauri, resigned after complaints that the 75–year old bureaucrat made persistent and improper advances to young woman who worked for him.

Pachauri was also the author of a somewhat explicit novel: *Return to Almora*. In the novel, an important bureaucrat, similar to Pachauri, has repeated explicitly described adventures of a romantic nature. The photo shows Pachauri (left) and an Indian government official displaying Pachauri's book.

Misbehavior of this type is a human failing, but the practitioners don't usually write explicit romance books. One has to ask if the head of the most important climate organization had a reckless personality, or at least a few loose screws.

---

[30]https://www.rossmckitrick.com/paleoclimatehockey-stick.html

The Nobel Prize and Al Gore

In 2007, the Nobel Peace Prize was awarded jointly to the IPCC and Al Gore, the former vice president of the U.S. The Nobel Peace Prize has little in common with the Nobel Prizes awarded for scientific achievement. The peace prize is awarded by a committee appointed by the Norwegian parliament. There is a long history of the prize being awarded to political activists, crackpots and frauds. For example, the Guatemalan activist Rigoberta Menchu received the 1992 prize. She was exposed as a fraud by the New York Times. Linus Pauling, a brilliant scientist, received the 1962 Peace Prize. He was a ban the bomb activist and was often considered a naive spokesman for Soviet Communism. In his later life, he promoted dubious theories, such as the theory that vitamin C prevents the common cold. Barack Obama was awarded the prize shortly after he was elected, and before he did anything, apparently because the Norwegians liked his speeches.

Al Gore created *An Inconvenient Truth*, a popular movie and book promoting global warming alarmism. The book was notable for having more than 25 photos of politician Al Gore. In the movie, Gore hogged the spotlight. Although professionally and expensively produced, the book and movie were filled with scientific errors.[31] Gore profited to the extent of several hundred million dollars from his crusade. The money was related to his prominence as a global warming promoter. He profited from the sale of a TV network he helped start as well as stock options from his service on the board of Apple Computer.

Climategate

In 2009 someone stole, and posted online, a large number of emails from the Climatic Research Unit of the University of East Anglia in the UK. These emails have been called Climategate. There were many emails between prominent scientists who are promoters of global warming alarmism. The emails revealed instances of suppressing opponents' publications. There was a

---

[31] English judge rules Al Gore's move has 9 errors.
http://www.telegraph.co.uk/news/earth/earthnews/3310137/Al-Gores-nine-Inconvenient-Untruths.html

cavalier attitude toward the norms of scientific research. The participants were obviously promoting a point of view, no matter what the scientific evidence was.[32] The critic John Costella wrote this:

> Climategate has shattered that [objectivity] myth. It gives us a peephole into the work of the scientists investigating arguably the most important issue ever to face mankind. Instead of seeing large collaborations of meticulous, careful, critical scientists, we instead see a small team of incompetent scientists; abusing almost every aspect of the framework of science to build a fence around themselves and their fellow activists, to prevent real scientists from seeing the shambles of their "research."

The global warming establishment worked quickly to contain the damage from the Climategate emails. Given support from the media and the scientific establishment, they succeeded. It is very hard to shake fanatic belief with facts or evidence. Khrushchev's secret speech revealing the corruption and brutality of Stalin caused many believing communists to defect. It would probably take a similar speech by James Hansen to do the same for global warming believers.

Sea Level Rise

One of the common global warming alarmist claims is that sea level is going to rise by a few feet to 20 feet. Global warming is supposed to melt glaciers, or even worse, melt the total Greenland ice cap. The photo below is an advertisement from the World Wildlife Fund that appeared at Liberty Airport in New Jersey. The implication of the advertisement is that sea level will rise and flood little league fields.

Currently sea level is rising 1–3 millimeters per year or 4–12 inches a century. It is hard to know exactly how much, as there are complaints that the data is tampered with by global warming advocates. Measuring sea level to within a few millimeters is

[32] The Climategate Emails and What They Mean, by John Costella. http://www.lavoisier.com.au/articles/greenhouse-science/climate-change/climategate-emails.pdf

complicated by the fact that the land bordering the ocean is often slowly rising or falling. due to the melting of the heavy ice age, ice sheets. When the last ice age melted, between 20,000 and 5,000 years ago, sea level rose 400 feet, or an average of about 31 inches per century.

There are two great ice sheets, Antarctica and Greenland. If the entire Greenland ice sheet melted sea level would rise another 20 feet. Melting of the Antarctica ice sheet is considered highly unlikely. The Greenland ice sheet has a volume of approximately 2.9 million cubic kilometers of ice. Based on short term measurements, by gravity measuring satellites, Greenland is losing about 200 cubic kilometers of ice per year. At that rate it would take 15,000 years to remove the entire ice sheet. If Greenland continues to lose ice at the current rate it would take 700 years for Greenland to contribute 1 foot of sea level rise. Greenland gains mass from snow and loses mass from ice melting and the plastic flow of ice toward the ocean. The climate of Greenland is volatile with cold and warm spells, so short-term measurements of the ice cap cannot be extrapolated into a trend. In the most recent measurement year, ending in August 2017, Greenland *gained* 44 cubic kilometers of ice. This could be random variation or the start of a new trend.

There are various low lying tropical islands that are only a few feet above sea level. There is plenty of propaganda claiming that these islands are in danger of being inundated by sea level rise. The inhabitants of the islands contribute to the clamor by demanding money and often visas to emigrate to more prosperous countries (the countries supposedly causing global warming) Virtually all the threatened islands are tropical islands sitting on coral. There are some puzzling aspects. How did these islands survive the 400 feet of sea level rise at the end of the ice age? Were these islands flat topped, 400-foot tall mountains when the ice age melt started? Then did the sea level rise just enough to leave 5 or 6 feet of these island sticking out above the water?

The solution to this puzzle is that as sea level rises the coral reefs in the water around the island grow. Coral polyps attach themselves to the reef under the water and grow, creating calcium carbonate (limestone) skeletons in the process. These living creatures create a kind of rock. Storms break up the coral rock and wash it up on the land. Perhaps wind-blown dust also settles on the islands. Plants growing on the islands provide organic matter that further bulks up the land. In any case, the islands are there, so the land must be growing upward, along with the coral under the sea surrounding the island. Apparently, the islands were able to grow fast enough to keep above the water when sea level was rising 31 inches per century during the ice age melt. Before we panic about these islands it might be prudent to wait for evidence that the sea is actually threatening the islands more than usual.

The island nation of Tuvalu is located in the tropical Pacific Ocean between Hawaii and Australia. A University of Auckland study, using aerial and satellite photography, found that the total land area of Tuvalu increased by 2.9 percent since 1971.[33] Tuvalu is often mentioned as one of the island nations supposedly threatened by global warming and rising sea level.

---

[33] Paul S. Kench et al. Patterns of island change and persistence offer alternate adaptation pathways for atoll nations, *Nature Communications* (2018).

The story of the coral islands is so obvious that the stories of upcoming inundation amount to denial of reality or a deliberate refusal to ignore well-known science.

Global Warming Science and Propaganda

Here are some of the biggest propaganda points of the global warming movement:

All scientists agree – A lie, pure and simple. Backed by fake polls.
The polar bears are dying – They are doing fine with increasing populations.
Record temperatures – Most U.S. warm temperature records were in the 1930's. Currently, global temperature has been increasing slowly compared to model predictions
Temperatures have shot up in the 20th century – This is the hockey stick thesis. Junk science. It was probably warmer in Medieval Warm Period during years 1000 to1400.

Some big scientific problems with the global warming thesis are the following:

The only temperature evidence supporting the CO_2 theory of global warming is the warming since about 1975. Prior to that there wasn't enough CO_2 growth in the atmosphere to have a substantial effect.

There is a strong alternative theory, promoted by the Danish scientist Hendrik Svensmark, that the Earth's climate is controlled, to some extent, by the Sun's magnetic field changing in synchronism with sunspots. The magnetic field modulates the number of cosmic rays impinging on the Earth's atmosphere. It is thought that the cosmic rays generate nuclei that encourage the formation of clouds. Clouds affect the amount of sunlight reaching the earth. Svensmark wrote a book: *The Chilling Stars: A Cosmic View of Climate Change*. The promoters of the CO_2 theory of global warming attack Svensmark relentlessly. I found Svensmark's 2009 scientific paper published in Geophysical Research Letters, "Cosmic Ray Decreases Affect Atmospheric Aerosols and Clouds" to be very convincing. In that paper he reports on the effects of so called Forbush events, natural events on the sun that affect cosmic ray fluxes.

The predictions of global warming come from computer models of the Earth's atmosphere. There are numerous problems with the models and with the way the models are combined to make predictions. Different models disagree with each other by a substantial amount. According to Kevin Trenberth, a model expert, and a very prominent climate scientist who is solidly on the side of the global warming promoters:

> ...none of the climate states in the models correspond even remotely to the current observed climate. In particular, the state of the oceans, sea ice, and soil moisture has no relationship to the observed state at any recent time in any of the IPCC models.[34]

Just because the models don't convincingly model the climate of the Earth doesn't prove that they are wrong in their predictions of global warming. But, it does create considerable doubt.

Like most of the imaginary impending catastrophes promoted by the environmental lobby, there is a kernel of real science in the global warming impending catastrophe. There are good reasons to expect that increasing CO_2 in the atmosphere will have a warming effect. Heat is carried away from the Earth by two processes: convection and radiation. In the lower atmosphere, convection dominates with rising and falling air masses. The temperature falls with increasing altitude at a rate known as the lapse rate. Above a certain level, known as the tropopause, infrared or heat radiation (infrared radiation is the radiation you feel coming from a hot stove) takes over as the mechanism for moving heat upward. Above the tropopause temperature does not fall with increasing altitude and convection cannot take place. Convection depends on rising hot air and sinking cool air. Convection is powered by a temperature gradient, that is, cooling with increased height. Without that gradient, there can be no convection. Adding CO_2 to the air

---

[34] http://blogs.nature.com/climatefeedback/2007/06/predictions_of_climate.html#more

above the tropopause increases resistance to outgoing radiation and causes the tropopause to rise a bit into thinner air where radiation resistance declines due to lower density of the air including CO_2. If the tropopause is higher the surface temperature has to be higher if the lapse rate that applies to convection remains the same. Put another way, the convection engine that moves heat upward has to move the heat further to the higher tropopause. The engine cannot move the required amount of heat unless the surface temperature is higher.

The theory is most convincing in isolation, but there are many other influences on climate. The lapse rate may change. The configuration of clouds may change, clouds having a strong effect on the Earth's energy balance. According to theory global warming should be faster at higher altitude in the tropics. This is known as the tropical hot spot. The problem is that the search for the tropical hot spot has largely failed, or at least is highly controversial. The implication of not finding the tropical hot spot is that the surface temperature is not increasing. The hot spot is seen when there are brief warming spells caused by the El Nino tropical pacific warming.

The IPCC models assume an amplifying effect due to increased temperature adding increased water vapor to the air, water vapor being a greenhouse gas. That assumption is also dubious, but critical to the global warming argument. The evidence is substantial that the models are inaccurate. Their behavior does not match that of the Earth, but even if did, it is difficult to pin the changes in climate to the greenhouse effect. The warming effect of CO_2 may be far less than claimed by the models. The global warming alarmists take a kernel of real science surrounded by uncertainty and turn speculation into a sure disaster.

The promoters of global warming will continue to believe in global warming alarmism no matter what the future temperature of the Earth does. Their financial futures are tied to global warming. There are many ways to dismiss temperature data that does not support the CO_2 caused global warming hypothesis. Prior to about 1975 the CO_2 effect is predicted to be small by the computer models. The recent, post 1975, temperature record is not very useful to prove or disprove greenhouse global warming because there are too many other things that can affect global temperature. Further these other effects mostly cannot be confidently measured or catalogued. An additional problem is that the global temperature is not well measured. The surface temperature measurements are particularly dubious. Satellite measurements are more trustworthy, but still have problems. For the last 20 years, as shown in the graph below, the amount of warming has been about 3 times less than the predictions of the IPCC and the computer models. The data below is from the University of Alabama group's satellite temperature, probably the most credible measurement of recent global temperature.

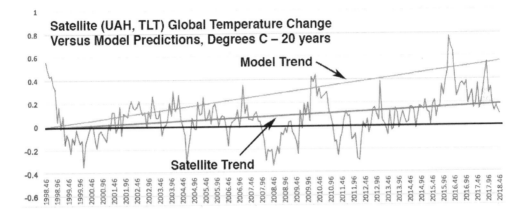

The *model trend* line in the graph is a surface temperature. The satellite temperature is not directly comparable because it rises faster in a rising temperature era. The satellite temperature is a measurement of a deep slice of the lower atmosphere about 5 miles thick. According to theory, the satellite temperature should increase faster[35] by 30–50% compared to the surface temperature. If we estimate the implied surface temperature from the satellite temperature, assuming a 30% acceleration, then the ratio between model predictions and estimated global surface temperature become 4 to 1 rather than 3 to 1. If global warming is four times slower than predicted, it becomes unimportant.

Surface measurements of global temperature is done by analyzing data from thousands of weather stations and other

---

[35] http://www.cfact.org/2016/01/26/measuring-global-temperatures-satellites-or-thermometers/

measurements of ocean data, often taken from ships. This surface temperature analysis suffers from lack of coverage of the Earth, changes in measuring techniques and instruments over the years, and political influence or confirmation bias effects. Confirmation bias refers to the psychological phenomenon of finding data to confirm one's beliefs. However, the surface temperature is all we have for years before 1979 when satellite measurements started.

The advocates of global warming can easily explain the warming deficit in various ways that are difficult to prove or dispute. For example, they can claim that the ocean is absorbing heat, or they can claim that aerosols in the atmosphere are absorbing sunlight. The warming that has been experienced cannot be firmly linked to global warming from greenhouse gases as there are still other things that can cause global warming or cooling. Anything in the temperature record can be further explained away by assuming that it is chaotic variation, the climate being a non-linear chaotic system. This uncertainty works both ways. If the temperature started to rapidly increase, it would not prove the CO_2 theory, because many things can cause global warming.

The advocates of global warming usually explain the hiatus or slow warming by claiming that heat is being absorbed by the oceans. Some scientists produced graphs purporting to show that the amount of heat stored in the upper 700 or 2000 meters of the oceans had increased by an appropriate amount. That is speculation, because there are other, unrelated to global warming, strong effects affecting upper ocean heat storage. A further complication is that much data produced by the advocates of global warming can't be trusted.

The ocean overturning circulation is a circulation created by cold and salty water sinking to the bottom of the ocean in the Arctic and Antarctic. The sinking water pushes up the ocean in an elevator like fashion, about four meters per year. The volume of sinking water is huge, much greater than the flow of any river. The temperature of approximately the top 100 meters of the oceans follows the air temperature. Below that *mixed layer*, the ocean gets progressively colder the deeper one goes (outside the polar regions). The ocean is colder below the mixed layer due to cold water that sunk to the bottom hundreds of years ago and that is rising on the elevator. The temperature of the upper ocean depends on downward heat flow from the atmosphere as well as the effects of mixing with colder deeper water.

Cold water sinking to the bottom of the ocean warms the upper ocean by moving colder than average water to the depths of the ocean. These effects are volatile, significant in scale, and poorly measured. As a consequence, the temperature of the upper 700 or 2000 meters of the ocean is not a good indicator of heat exchange with the ocean. If the heat content of the entire ocean could be measured, that would be a better indicator of heat storage in the oceans. Measuring the heat content of the ocean is challenging, involving robotic floats and temperature measurements accurate to thousandths of a degree C.

The fact that there was a 1910 to 1940 warming stronger than the 1970 to 1998 warming blows a big hole in the CO_2 theory because the early warming took place without significant help from CO_2. No one knows what caused that early warming.

I have made a case that it is difficult to use the fact of weak warming to prove that global warming alarmism is wrong. The advocates can say that not only was the warming caused by CO_2 but that it would have been greater except for some countervailing force like ocean heat absorption or chaotic variations. They are perfectly correct. Using recent weak warming to disprove the CO_2 theory is dubious. They seem to forget that the opposite holds true when they tout increasing temperature as if it proves their case.

The constant claims that the science is solid and that we must listen to science are simply childish nonsense. The science is speculation made to seem impressive by means of extremely complicated computer programs.

I have only scratched the surface of the mountain of evidence that global warming prospects are highly uncertain and probably exaggerated. The positive effects of CO_2 for plants are not in question.

Advocates of global warming alarmism bring up the *precautionary principle* – the idea that we should take action now against global warming as a precaution because even if there is a small chance of catastrophic global warming, the consequences would be very serious. The trouble with this is that we could soon be wasting a lot of energy chasing imaginary threats. There are many real threats that are better understood than global warming, yet nothing is being done about those threats. For example, why don't we have blast shelters against nuclear war for the entire population, like Switzerland. Why don't we have a robust capability to intercept asteroids headed for collision with the Earth? Why don't we have a plan to stop a smallpox epidemic given that the virus is still in freezers in the U.S. and Russia, as well as potentially present in bodies buried in the Arctic? Why is the electric grid not protected against electromagnetic pulse? Unlike these threats, global warming, if it materializes, would be a slow change.

The biggest reason for doubting global warming alarmism is that the scientific establishment and environmental organizations pushing the theory are heavily invested, financially and ideologically, in the theory. If the theory falls by the wayside, so do the careers of the people working in these areas. In any case, as has been made clear here, wind and solar are not logical solutions for worry about global warming. Nuclear power is the logical solution, as some of the most prominent promoters of global warming alarmism have pointed out.

The Role of Amateur Scientists

A striking feature of the global warming debate is the role of amateur scientists. These are people who take on the professional scientific bureaucracy. Most have scientific or engineering educations. The rise of the Internet has made it possible for them to propagate their ideas via websites, free of the stranglehold of the mass media.

The amateurs are retired or have jobs outside of professional science. As a result, they can speak freely, unlike professional scientists who worry about retaliation if they criticize global warming dogma. The downside is that they are amateurs and as a consequence may make mistakes due to lack of an extensive specialized education in climate related matters.

Prior to the 20th century, many scientists were amateur's dependent on wealthy benefactors or some other source of income. Einstein had a job as a patent examiner with the Swiss patent office. The Mount Palomar telescope, completed in 1949 and for many years the largest in the world, was built with private money supplied by the Rockefellers. The huge expansion of science as a paid profession was driven by the World War II and the later Cold War.

The massive government involvement in science has made it difficult for professional scientists to make criticisms that endanger government funding.

The *Global Warming Petition Project* circulated a petition on the Internet rejecting global warming theory. Over 30,000 people signed the petition including over 9,000 with doctoral degrees. The petition was supported by Frederick Seitz a very prominent scientist. Arthur B. Robinson, a controversial figure and former associate of Linus Pauling, devised the petition and manages it from his headquarters in Cave Junction, Oregon. Robinson is a biochemist who broke with the scientific establishment and started he own lab in rural Oregon.

The amateur scientist Steve McIntyre, a semi-retired Canadian mining consultant, is one of the most remarkable and distinguished amateur scientists. Obviously mathematically talented, McIntyre finished first in the Canadian high school mathematics competition in 1965. He runs a website: Climateaudit.org. The flavor of McIntyre's commentary is shown by this recent excerpt:

> Recently a new model-based paper on climate sensitivity was published by Kate Marvel, Gavin Schmidt (the head of NASA GISS) and others, titled 'Internal variability and disequilibrium confound estimates of climate sensitivity from observations'. It appears to me that the novel part of its analysis is faulty, and that the part which isn't faulty isn't novel.

McIntyre greatly outclasses the professional climate scientists, especially on statistical issues. His commentary features dry humor. He is most famous for demolishing the hockey stick graph that claimed temperature is dramatically increasing in the 20th century

Anthony Watts runs the web site Wattsupwiththat.com. Watts has a background as a TV meteorologist and an electrical engineer, but apparently, no college degree. He has a company that makes various equipment related to weather. His website is extremely popular and generally features articles critical of global warming. Watts made an important contribution when he organized a survey of U.S. Weather stations that showed many being poorly located; for example, near air conditioner outlets that exhaust hot air.

Tony Heller runs a website realclimatescience.com, called *The Deplorable Climate Science Blog*. According to the pro-global warming site DeSmogBlog, Heller has a master's degree in electrical engineering and an undergraduate degree in geology. He specializes in exposing tampering with climate data by the global warming establishment.

There are numerous other sites, many of excellent quality. My own sites are climateviews.com and DumbEnergy.com.

Unfortunately, there are also sites that oppose global warming but propagate poor science. In my opinion a site that fits this description is principia-scientific.org. For example, there is an article on the site claiming that the greenhouse effect does not exist and violates the laws of thermodynamics.

Is There a Nuclear Future?

Nuclear energy is well suited for the generation of electricity. Compared to wind and solar, nuclear is better – CO_2-free, reliable and dispatchable, low cost fuel, endless supply of fuel, and no air pollution. Nuclear is the greatest potential competitor to wind and solar for reducing CO_2 emissions.

Nuclear energy has great promise. That promise is weakened by aggressive political opposition. There are sincere reasons to be worried about nuclear power – the possibility of a release of radioactivity and the possibility of civilian nuclear power being used as a route to nuclear bombs. But the usual suspects – Environmental organizations and green ideologues – are not interested having an even-handed discussion.

The energy available from nuclear fission is vast in comparison to the energy released by burning fossil fuels. A large nuclear plant generating 1000 megawatts consumes about 25 tons of enriched uranium fuel per year. An equivalent coal plant would consume 3 million tons of coal per year. The ratio of the weight of the fuel is more than a hundred thousand to one. To provide fuel for the 1000-megawatt coal plant, a coal train has to arrive every other day.

The fuel for nuclear reactors is very concentrated and very cheap. At recent prices nuclear fuel costs about 3/4ths cent per kWh; less than half the cost of fuel for the most efficient natural gas or coal plants. Typically, a power reactor only needs to be refueled every 18 months, replacing 1/3 of the fuel at each refueling. Nuclear reactors can pass through disruptions in fuel delivery that cripple traditional plants, continuing to operate for many months without refueling. A coal plant may have enough fuel on hand for 30 days. A natural gas plant will go down when the pipeline goes down, unless it is a dual fuel plant with a tank of oil on the site. That tank of oil probably won't last very long.

About 20 percent of U.S. electricity comes from nuclear. Those plants were built years ago. According to Wikipedia, in the U.S., only one new reactor has begun commercial operation since 1996. That 20 percent of U.S. electricity comes from reactors built 30 or 40 years ago.

Millstone 1 Nuclear Power Plant
660 megawatts Cost $101 million 1966

Millstone 1, near New London, CT was constructed in 5 years and operated from 1970 to 1998. Two other reactors, units 2 and 3 are still operating on the site.

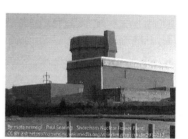

Shoreham Nuclear Power Plant
820 megawatts cost $6 billion 1973

The Shoreham plant on Long Island, NY was under construction for 11 years. In June, 1979 thousands of protestors gathered at the plant and 500 were arrested. The plant was finally scrapped In 1989 and never generated electricity.

Nuclear Cost Escalation

The same environmental organizations promoting wind and solar to save us from global warming are largely responsible for destroying the carbon-free, nuclear electricity industry in the U.S.A. Even though nuclear emits no CO_2, the environmentalists hate it. They hate it because in the 1970s and 1980s nuclear was their pet target that they used to fill a slot in the parade of impending catastrophes needed to keep their organizations in the black.

An Australian economist, Peter Lang, wrote a paper[36] suggesting that Nuclear Energy followed the normal development progression for new technologies of declining costs and increased adaption until political opposition stopped the progression and caused costs to rapidly increase, rather than continue to decrease. The loss to the world economy caused by environmental organizations attacking nuclear power with a storm of hysterical lies is very great. The loss is particularly great in the U.S. where the industry originated and had great potential. What could have been a major U.S. industry is thriving in South Korea and China.

Nuclear Economics

Nuclear suffers from poor economics in the U.S. The capital cost has been driven up by barrels of red tape inspired by the sustained attack of the environmentalists. The arrival of plentiful and cheap natural gas from fracking has made natural gas into a formidable competitor.

In the U.S., the capital cost of reactors is about $6,000 per kW of capacity. With an 8 percent discount rate, 40-year life and 90 percent capacity factor, that translates into a capital cost of about 6.4 cents per kWh. In South Korea reactors are built for $2,500 per kW, making the capital cost is about 2.5 cents per kWh. The Korean cost is competitive with gas, especially in South Korea where the gas is imported as LNG and may cost 2-3 times more than in the U.S. South Korea's electricity is more than 30 percent nuclear. The rest is from imported coal and gas.

According to Wikipedia, China has 38 nuclear reactors with 18 units under construction. There are two units under construction in the U.S. while 34 units have been closed down

---

[36] Nuclear Power Learning and Deployment Rates; Disruption and Global Benefits Forgone. Peter Lang in Energies. *www.mdpi.com/1996-1073/10/12/2169/pdf*

for good. Nuclear has a greater appeal in Asian countries lacking sufficient domestic fossil fuels.

Nuclear reactors are divided into 4 generations. Most current reactors are generation II with generation III reactors just entering service or under construction. Generation III reactors are expected to be cheaper due to design simplifications. Generation IV reactors are expected in the 2020's. Most nuclear activity is overseas. The U.S. nuclear industry has been largely destroyed by environmental activism. The destruction of the nuclear industry, in the country where it was invented, was complete long before cheap natural gas from fracking arrived. (The environmentalists are now busy trying to destroy the coal industry in the United States.)

A problem with nuclear reactors is that when they are temporarily shut down, they continue to produce considerable heat due to short-lived and "hot" radioactive isotopes in the core. The amount of heat declines quickly as the isotopes decay, but if the core is not cooled for a period after the shutdown, it will get very hot and melts, resulting in the destruction of the reactor. After shutdown, pumps circulate cooling water through the core. If the grid is down, then emergency generators provide power for the pumps. After the recent earthquake in Japan, a tsunami flooded and disabled the emergency generators, resulting in core meltdowns. Generation III reactors use a passive emergency cooling system using heat-driven, convective circulation that requires no electricity. This is both a safety feature and a simplification.

Generation III reactors are also designed for load following. That means that their power output can be increased and decreased to follow demand. Generation II reactors, at least in the U.S., are operated as baseload generators, always operating at full power. Load following allows reactors to be a larger portion of the grid, increasing power to handle daytime peaks and reducing power generation at night.

Beyond generations I–IV of light water[37] reactors there are many possibilities, backed by sound theory, but having engineering challenges.

There are two isotopes[38] of natural uranium, U235 and U238. Only U235, less than 1 percent of natural uranium, serves as fuel. But U238 can be converted into plutonium, another element that can also serve as fuel. All reactors convert some of the U238 in their core to plutonium, but reactors of a special design can generate more plutonium fuel than they consume U235 fuel. These are called breeder reactors. Breeder reactors effectively multiply the amount of nuclear fuel by a factor of more than 50. Although uranium is fairly plentiful, with breeding, the potential fuel supply becomes vast. Breeder reactors can also burn up nuclear waste as fuel, an economic benefit. Although breeder reactors have been successfully operated for years, they are not yet commercially viable. More engineering work is needed.

Another radioactive element is thorium. Thorium is more plentiful than uranium. It cannot directly fuel a reactor, but it can be bred into uranium, U233, an isotope of uranium not occurring in nature, but a good reactor fuel. A thorium fueled reactor needs to be started with uranium or plutonium, but once started enough U233 can be generated to keep it going without replenishment. Thorium reactors have various advantages and problems. Various experimental reactors using Thorium have been built and operated.

Another experimental reactor is the small modular reactor. These small reactors, maybe 25 megawatts, could be built in a factory, transported to a site and buried. Modular reactors might be designed for infrequent refueling. Such a reactor could be

---

[37] Light water is regular water. Heavy water is water in which the hydrogen is heavy hydrogen, called deuterium. Deuterium is a naturally-occurring, isotope of hydrogen, with a neutron added to the nucleus. Deuterium has less tendency to absorb neutrons and thus is a superior coolant and moderator for a reactor, allowing the reactor to operate on non-enriched, natural uranium. Heavy water reactors are a minor branch of reactor technology, but prominent for manufacturing plutonium for nuclear weapons.
[38] Isotopes of elements are different versions of the same element have more or fewer neutrons in the nucleus. Different isotopes of the same element are the same chemically, but slightly different in their nuclear properties.

very cost effective and very safe. Multiple modular reactors could be ganged together to construct larger power stations.

Another experimental reactor, is the molten salt reactor. They use fuel in the form of a liquid salt. An advantage is that if the reactor overheats a drain plug would melt and drain the fuel to a safe place where it could cool down without creating damage. Molten salt reactors have been built and operated on an experimental basis.

Nuclear Safety

Environmental pressure groups have built a culture of hysteria around radioactivity. Radioactivity is part of our natural surroundings and the human body has evolved a tolerance for it. There has only been one nuclear reactor accident that exposed a significant number of people to radiation. That was the destruction of the Chernobyl reactor in the Soviet Union in 1986. That particular reactor had no containment vessel and was operated in a very careless fashion. The core contained a large quantity of graphite bricks that served as a moderator to aid in conditioning the neutrons in the reaction. Unfortunately, graphite, being carbon, like coal, is flammable and the bricks caught fire, spreading radioactive substances into the atmosphere. The Chernobyl accident was a worst case nuclear accident. As a consequence of this worst-case accident 31 people were killed. Approximately 4,000 people got thyroid cancer. That cancer is highly treatable and there were only 9 deaths. If the Soviets had promptly distributed iodine pills, most of those cancers would have been prevented. In future years, several thousand more people may die prematurely of cancer, but that effect is difficult to detect and speculative due to the much larger number of natural cancer deaths.

Contrast the deaths from the Chernobyl accident with 40,000 deaths per year in the U.S. from auto accidents, or 135,000 deaths from lung cancer caused by smoking. Around a dozen coal miners die in accidents each year in the U.S. Worldwide probably more than 5,000 people are killed each year in coal mining accidents. Coal is a principal alternative to nuclear energy.

In the U.S. there have been nuclear accidents in the power industry, but never a significant release of radiation and very few deaths. For those who are worried about emissions of CO_2, nuclear is the answer.

The bottom line is that nuclear reactors are safe and have an excellent track record. The new generations of reactors will be even safer. The money spent on renewable energy would be better spent on nuclear energy and research into better nuclear energy.

There are a lot of things in this world that can kill large numbers of people. Nuclear bombs are obvious ones. Nuclear reactors have limited potential for mass killing as demonstrated by the Chernobyl accident. Nerve gas is much easier to make than nuclear bombs and has a large potential for killing people. A 1968 nerve gas accident in Utah killed 6,000 sheep. The Japanese doomsday cult, Aum Shinrikyo, manufactured sarin gas and released it in the Tokyo subway in 1995. Fortunately, only 13 people were killed. Other methods of mass murder are blowing up dams or releasing exotic diseases in crowded cities.

The much discussed "dirty bomb" is mainly a psychological weapon. The idea of a dirty bomb is to use chemical explosives to disperse radioactive material in a city. The problem is that to gather enough hot radioactive material to make the bomb dangerous is not feasible, not only be because the radioactivity would be dangerous, but because the material would too (thermally) hot to handle. However due to the fear of radioactivity fanned by decades of hysterical propaganda, the psychological effect would be great. The radioactivity could be easily reduced to harmless levels by washing the material away with fire hoses. However, due to the fear of radioactivity fanned by decades of hysterical propaganda, the psychological effect would be great. (The explosion of a dirty bomb would present a great opportunity to buy real estate cheaply.)

Radiation is dangerous in large quantities. The danger of low level radiation is controversial. Like global warming the danger of low level radiation is based on theoretical models. The theoretical model, known as the linear, no threshold (LNT) model, predicts that even low levels of radiation are dangerous, even radiation emitted everywhere by the Earth and known as background radiation. The LNT model has been called into question. There is substantial evidence based on actual radiation exposure that the model is wrong. But, great mental inertia is invested in the old paradigm of radiation danger.[39]

Proliferation of Nuclear Weapons

Civilian reactors designed for generating electricity are a possible source of plutonium for bombs. There are a number of practical barriers as well as international inspection regimes that make it difficult, but not impossible, to utilize the reactors for bomb making purposes. The plutonium normally produced in civilian reactors is unsuitable for use in bombs because too much of the contaminant (from the perspective of bomb making) Pu-240 is produced in civilian reactors. The Pu-240 leads to bombs that fizzle out rather than having a large explosive yield. Preventing proliferation of nuclear weapons is a political problem, not a technical problem. If the major powers are determined to stop proliferation, it can be done. A rouge state cannot build bombs in total secrecy because of the industrial facilities and special equipment that is needed.

---

[39] For more on this see my articles at climateviews.com: *Forbidden Science: Low Level Radiation and Cancer* and the article *Fighting Junk Science.*

The Benefits of CO$_2$

Without carbon dioxide in the atmosphere there would be no life on Earth. Plants breathe CO$_2$ and all animal life is ultimately dependent upon plant life. The quantity of CO$_2$ in the atmosphere is very small, one molecule in 2500. Plants are constantly clawing CO$_2$ out of the atmosphere so that they can grow. Adding CO2 to the atmosphere causes crops to grow better and deserts to recede.

Plant Metabolism

Plants combine CO$_2$ and water (H$_2$O) in order to create their bodies, made of hydrocarbon compounds. By using the sun's energy and the process of photosynthesis, the plants take carbon from the CO$_2$ and hydrogen from the H$_2$0. The oxygen (O) that is left over is exhaled. If it weren't for photosynthesis the oxygen in the atmosphere might be slowly consumed by the formation of oxygen compounds. We live on food derived from plants. We eat food that is oxidized in our bodies to provide energy. We breathe out CO$_2$. The cycle of life on Earth gets its energy at bottom from photosynthesis, driven by sunlight. Of course, sunlight is from nuclear reactions in the Sun.

Fossil fuels, such as coal, oil and natural gas, are the result of plants that grew long ago and were buried. Over time the plant bodies turn into one of the fossil fuels. The fossil fuels are made of hydrogen and carbon. Coal has the most carbon and the least hydrogen, Natural gas has the most hydrogen and the least carbon. Oil is in between.

If plants live in an atmosphere enriched in CO_2, most plants grow faster and use less water. The reason they use less water is that plants have pores on their leaves called stomata, through which they take in CO_2. The stomata can open and close. When photosynthesis takes place, the plant takes in CO_2 and breathes out oxygen. Plants get water from their roots. An undesirable side effect of open stomata is that water escapes via evaporation. Because water is lost via the open stomata, the plant will close the stomata to conserve water if conditions are dry. The stomata close at night because photosynthesis cannot take place without sunlight. If the atmosphere is enriched with CO_2, the plants can obtain needed CO_2 with less water loss.

385   535   685   835
Growth of Eldarica Pine trees under varying degrees of CO2 atmosphere enrichment parts per million, ambient 385ppm to 835ppm. Photo: Craig Idso.

Plants are categorized by the way they use carbon. The plants are either C3, C4 or CAM plants. CAM plants are mostly desert plants that are not economically important. Most plants are C3 plants. There are only 86 species of C4 plants of which 4 are economically important: corn, sorghum, millet and sugarcane. Many important crops are C3 plants. C4 plants are less sensitive to CO_2 enrichment, but enriching CO_2 does decrease their water use. C3 plants both grow faster and use less water if the atmosphere is enriched in CO_2.

Effect of CO_2 Levels on Crops

The photo above shows the effect on the rate of growth of a tree from various levels of CO_2 enrichment, from ambient (about 385 parts per million when the photo was taken) to +450 parts per million (more than double).

A satellite study has found that increased CO_2 in the atmosphere has created extensive greening of the Earth.[40] Greenhouses are often equipped with CO_2 generators to increase the growth of plants.

In an experiment in India rice and corn were grown under ambient (400 ppm) and enriched CO_2 (550 ppm). About a 10 percent improvement in yield was experienced for both crops.

The CO_2 Coalition (co2coalition.org) has information on the benefits of CO_2.

---

[40] Carbon Dioxide Fertilization Greening Earth, Study Finds
https://www.nasa.gov/feature/goddard/2016/carbon-dioxide-fertilization-greening-earth

How the Grid Works

With the exception of solar photovoltaic, the grid is powered by massive rotating machinery. A turbine driven by moving gas, or moving water, drives a generator that generates electricity. The photo below is from a 600-megawatt coal generating station in Arkansas. The turbine is on the right and the generator is on the left. This turbine is driven by high pressure steam generated by burning coal. Look at the people on the right side of the photo for scale.

There are excellent YouTube videos that explain turbines and generators in detail.

An electrical grid (there are 3 major grids in the U.S.) uses dozens or hundreds of generating plants that together provide the electricity for the millions of electricity users connected to the grid. The output of all the generating plants together has to match the electrical load from all the users of electricity. The match does not have to be perfectly exact because the grid will automatically, to some extent, reallocate power between users as the load changes. Most of the generators are synchronized with each other and with the 60-cycle frequency of the alternating current on the grid. Usually generators revolve at

3600 revolutions per minute. Wind turbines are an exception as they use a different type of generator.

If the load increases the generators start to struggle and they slow down a little bit. That causes the frequency of the electricity on the grid to decrease. The frequency change is detected and corrective action is taken to increase output. The corrective action may be automatic or initiated by human intervention.

In order to increase output, generating plants that are not at full power might increase power. Another way to increase power is to start up idle generator plants that are in reserve. If output cannot be increased, then electricity users are progressively cut off. If everything goes wrong, there will be a blackout.

In the opposite case, if the load decreases then the frequency will increase, and output power of the generators must be decreased.

Because there are thousands of users connected to the grid and dozens or hundreds of generators, these changes tend to be gradual and to some extent predictable. Unpredictable changes can happen if a large generator trips and goes off line for some reason. Sufficient reserve capacity, called spinning reserve, is kept ready to handle such contingencies.

Most generating stations need to draw power from the grid in order to start up their turbines. The amount of power needed to start one generating plant can be substantial, often dozens of megawatts. If there is a blackout, generators dependent on the grid for startup power can't be started. Certain plants, known as black start plants, are able to start up when the grid is down. Those plants have local emergency power sources to provide the power to start the main turbines. To restore the grid after a blackout, the black start plants start up first to provide power to the plants that can't start by themselves. The process goes step by step and can take hours. If transmission paths are dysfunctional, perhaps due to damaged transformers, then startup power from the black start plants to the non–black start plants may be blocked.

In order to transport electricity long distances, transformers are used to step up and step down the voltage. For example, the voltage entering a house is typically 240 volts that can be connected as 2 circuits of 120 volts. Electricity is distributed around neighborhoods at a voltage of about 4000 volts. For transporting electricity hundreds of miles, voltages from 115,000 to 765,000 volts are used.

In order to transmit more power on a wire, either the wire can be made fatter or the electrical voltage can be made higher. For long distances the voltage is always boosted up by a transformer. At the destination, the voltage is stepped down by another transformer to a more convenient level.

A transformer utilizes a magnetic iron core with coils of wire wrapped around the core. Transformers efficiently change the voltage of the electricity with very little loss of energy. Transformers used by utilities vary from the size of a waste can to the size of a house.

When it is necessary to transport electricity further than 800 or 1000 miles, different and more expensive *direct current* is used.

An expense associated with wind or solar is the cost of the transmission lines from remote locations where the installation is located to locations where the electricity is used. For example, in Texas the wind resource is located in the west, 500 miles away from the population centers where the electricity is needed. Special power lines had to be constructed at a cost of billions to make it possible to use the wind electricity. About 20 percent of the electricity was lost on that long trip.

Power lines that carry wind or solar power have to be sized to carry the maximum output, but the average output is about 1/3rd of the maximum output. The result is that the power line is expensive for the amount of power it actually transports.

Neither wind nor solar power is emergency power. They don't work unless the grid is already working.

The Destruction of the Grid

There are three power grids in the continental U.S., one in the west, one in the east and one in Texas. Within each grid the generators are synchronized to run at the same frequency. These 3 grids make up the national grid, including parts of Canada. If a grid, or part of a grid fails, economic activity stops and billions of dollars of economic activity is lost. If the entire national grid, or a major part of the national grid, were to fail for an extended period, the consequences would be disastrous. Distribution of food and fuel would be difficult. A failure in winter would cause most space heating to fail because even if the heat does not come from electricity, the equipment and controls are powered by electricity.

In principle it would be possible for the population to survive an extended failure of the national grid. Certainly, there is plenty of food in the form of corn and soybeans stored in the Midwest. There are also 80 million live cattle. There is potentially enough fuel oil to power trains and trucks to transport critical goods.

The problem is that there are inadequate preparations. Emergency generators often only have onsite fuel for only 24 hours. A system for allocating and distributing fuel is needed. There has to be a system for feeding the population when electricity is lost. Sewer and water systems must continue to work. There must be readily available supplies of food and water stored locally to keep the population fed until rudimentary food distribution can be resumed. The military and police must continue to operate.

Temporary grid failures, lasting up to 24 hours have taken place. As a consequence of hurricanes localized grid failure of days or weeks have taken place.

There are certain components of the grid that cannot be replaced quickly. The most vulnerable capital equipment is the giant transformers that are needed to transport electricity for long distances. These transformers, often as big as a house, are largely manufactured overseas, and have to be ordered many months in advance.

The Northeast blackout of August, 2003 affected 55 million people in the U.S. and Canada. For most people the blackout lasted for about 24 hours. The 2003 blackout was a cascading blackout. An overloaded power line automatically switched off, redirecting power to other paths that also became overloaded and shut down. Grid operators were unable to respond effectively, partly because a software bug blinded them to what was happening. In a few locations islands of power survived because operators were able to isolate the island from the grid.

The longer a blackout continues the more difficult it becomes to recover and the more serious the consequences are.[41] For example many electric grid substations lose backup power after 8-16 hours. Without backup power the substations cannot be remotely controlled and a technician has to go to the station to manually open and close the circuit breakers. After 24 hours the cellphone systems are likely to lose backup power and fail. After 5 days grid control rooms may lose backup power. After 7 days nuclear plant backup generators will run out of fuel. Nuclear plants are always shut down according to regulation if the grid is failing. If the backup generator fuel is not

---

[41] The information in this paragraph is from the testimony of Thomas Popik, the president of the Foundation for Resilient Societies before the Federal energy Regulatory Commission June 22, 2017.

replenished, core cooling will fail and a core meltdown will happen. Without power the cooling for spent fuel pools will stop and the pools will boil, eventually going dry and creating a radiation disaster. Clearly, the longer the blackout, the more difficult it will be to recover.

Excepting hurricane regions, few gas stations have backup power. That means that they can't pump gas. As a result, motorists will run out of gas and create traffic problems. In congested areas traffic lights will fail, further aggravating traffic. Many people use credit cards and carry little cash. As a result, if the credit card system fails, they will be unable to purchase anything.

Not all sewer plants and water purification plants have full backup power. As a result, raw sewage may be released or backup on to city streets. Water pressure may fail or the water may become unsanitary.

Of course, every effort should be made to prevent grid failure, but we also have to be prepared for a grid failure. Preparation means having adequate backup power and having a robust system for refueling backup generators for as long as necessary.

In northern regions during the winter heating will be a severe problem. Even if the natural gas distribution is working, most heaters won't work due to lack of electricity. Without heat pipes may freeze causing widespread damage if the pipes burst. Without heat and depending on the temperature, some people will suffer from hypothermia or even freeze to death. The advantages of wood or propane stoves are obvious in such circumstances.

Most grid failures have been accidental and limited. For example, a power line sags due to heating when run under heavy load and touches a tree. Then the power line is automatically tripped off line. That situation set off the 2003 northeast blackout.

A massive blackout could be caused by a natural, solar geomagnetic storm, or by deliberate sabotage. The sabotage could be by a terrorist group or by a nation state. The method of sabotage could be a physical attack on equipment, a cyber-attack or a high altitude nuclear explosion.

A solar geomagnetic storm[42] is caused by an ejection of a mass of plasma from the sun that travels toward the Earth and interacts with the Earth's magnetic field. This causes a change in the Earth's magnetic field that passes underneath long transmission lines. The changing magnetic field induces a direct current in the transmission line. Except for certain specialized transmission lines, transmission lines normally carry only alternating current that reverses positive and negative polarity 60 times a second (60 in the U.S., 50 in some other countries). The direct current induced by a geomagnetic storm is superimposed on the normal alternating current and when it passes through the transformer at the end of the power line. The direct current acts as poison to the transformer.

The high voltage transformers at the terminus of long transmission lines use a type of magnetic material made of special iron. The iron stores the energy in a magnetic field as an intermediate between the input and output of the transformer. Wire carrying current is wound around the iron core. However, the iron core can only sustain a magnetic field up to a certain strength. When that intensity of magnetic field is reached, the magnetic material becomes resistant to storing more energy. The core is said to be saturated. If the core saturates the transformer overheats and may even melt. Enough direct current drives the core into saturation. That is why direct current is a poison to the transformer. Even if the transformer does not fail immediately, it may be damaged by overheating and fail a few weeks later.

The large high voltage transformers are massive and expensive pieces of capital equipment that must be ordered from mostly overseas suppliers months or years in advance. The longer the transmission line the greater the danger. There are methods of protecting the transformers from this danger, but little has been done.

---

[42] See: Impacts of Severe Space Weather on the Electric Grid, The MITRE Corporation, JSR-11-320 November 2011.

The most intense geomagnetic storm we know of was the Carrington Event in 1859. The electrical grid did not exist at that time, but telegraph lines were severely affected.

In March 1989, a strong geomagnetic storm collapsed the Quebec grid. Two transformers were destroyed indirectly by Direct Current that caused protective devices to malfunction. The failure of a transformer in New Jersey sometime later, was also a consequence of that event.

A nuclear weapon can be used to create an electromagnetic pulse (EMP) that creates a broad spectrum of damage to electrical devices, including damage to long transmission lines and their associated transformers. If a nuclear weapon is exploded in near outer space, say 200 miles above Kansas, it can create an electromagnetic pulse affecting the entire continental U.S. A weapon exploded in outer space will create a flash in the sky, but no shockwave or significant radiation will reach the ground. No person or building will be damaged by the explosion. But the gamma rays emitted from the weapon will travel toward the earth and interact with the Earth's atmosphere. The plentiful and energetic gamma rays will knock electrons off atoms in the thin, high atmosphere and impart a high velocity to the electrons. The electrons will travel in a spiral path around the magnetic lines of force of the Earth's magnetic field. The spiraling electrons will emit a powerful electromagnetic pulse that will travel to the ground.

The initial pulse will be very sharp and very powerful. Large voltages will be induced in equipment like computers, possibly damaging critical components. The potential is to damage computers and electronic equipment used to control the grid. If a large amount of computer and communications equipment is suddenly taken out of service, the results are not likely to be pretty.

The initial sharp pulse is followed by weaker disturbances including magnetic effects that can induce direct currents much like a geomagnetic storm, but often even stronger.

Equipment can be protected against a nuclear electromagnetic pulse (EMP). For protection, equipment is enclosed in metal boxes with protective filters on wires entering and leaving the box. Entire rooms can be protected in the same way. The military have long been aware of EMP and critical military equipment is hardened against EMP. In the case of an EMP attack our missiles and planes should still work, as well as the communications equipment involved. So, if North Korea damages our grid and electronic infrastructure with an EMP attack, we can still destroy North Korea. Destroying North Korea will not help the U.S. population deprived of electricity for months or years.

There have only been a few tests of nuclear weapons in outer space, in the 1960's. Those tests were not well instrumented to record the EMP effects that were not expected to be as strong as they turned out to be. The most interesting tests were in the Soviet Union, so only incomplete information is available. In addition, much of the information that we do have is classified and not publicly available. Estimates of the effect of an EMP attack are based on computer models. (Not all computer models are bad but using computer models rather than experiments introduces uncertainty.)

A weapon used to execute an EMP attack is not necessarily a powerful weapon. Special design weapons would be most effective for creating EMP. Presumably such a weapon would have high gamma ray emissions. It is suspected that the North Koreans possess the design of such a weapon, possibly obtained from a Soviet weapons expert.

An EMP attack against the United States is most attractive for small, hostile nuclear powers. North Korea and Iran are the most likely candidates. Unfortunately, is it much easier for our enemies to get such a weapon than it is for us to defend against it. This points up the urgency of preventing North Korea from obtaining missiles suitable for such an attack. In any case, critical infrastructure should be hardened against EMP.

Physical attack and cyber-attack are other methods of attacking the grid.

There have been physical attacks on electric substations. The Metcalf substation, south of San Jose, California, was attacked with rifles in 2013. The attackers cut telephone lines that could signal an alarm and then shot over 100 rounds into transformers knocking many of the transformers offline and causing millions of dollars in damage.

Natural Gas Pipeline AZ to CA at Colorado River

In 2016 a substation near Kanab Utah was attacked with a rifle. The cooling radiator for a transformer was punctured and the transformer overheated and failed. The damage was $1 million. A temporary portable transformer was installed while repairs that were said to require 6-months were performed.

Substations are unattended and protected by little more than a chain link fence. Power lines are easy targets because they typically run through remote and unpopulated areas. Natural gas pipelines are similar targets. In many places, such as California, the electricity generation system is heavily dependent on just in time delivery of natural gas. Both high voltage lines and natural gas pipelines have been attacked many times with firearms, mostly by vandals or protesters. Power lines have been brought down by rifle shots.

Cyber-attacks on the electrical grid are a serious possibility. During the Russian-Ukrainian war the Ukrainian grid was blacked out on many occasions by hacking attacks.[43] The software used was very sophisticated. Software bombs can be planted in grid computers, set to go off at a certain time in the future. The software can be used to physically destroy grid equipment. In the Ukraine attacks it seems that the Russians showed restraint and did not try to physically destroy the Ukrainian grid by cyber-attack.

Physical destruction of grid equipment can be achieved by disabling protective devices and by operating equipment in abnormal ways. The Aurora Vulnerability was demonstrated in a 2007 test at the Idaho National Laboratory.[44] By disconnecting and reconnecting a rotating machine, such as a power plant generator, the machine can be destroyed. When synchronism with the grid is broken, the machine is subject to extreme physical and electrical stress. The cyber attacker needs to get control of a circuit breaker connecting the machine to the grid and manipulate it to break synchronism. Although there are devices available to protect against the Aurora Vulnerability, little has been done.

The Stuxnet virus was used to attack a uranium enrichment plant in Iran. Stuxnet was probably devised by the U.S. and Israel. Stuxnet incorporated techniques that could also be used to attack the electric grid. The Stuxnet virus attacked a particular type of Siemens programmable logic controller that was used to control the centrifuges used to enrich uranium. Enriching uranium is a first step to building nuclear weapons. Programmable logic controllers are a type of computer specialized for the control of industrial machinery. Programmable logic controllers are used extensively to control the infrastructure of the electric grid. The Iranian equipment was disconnected from the Internet, but the virus was infiltrated by infecting equipment bought into the plant.

---

[43] Wired Magazine Crash Override: The Malware That Took Down A Power Grid. Andy Greenberg 6/12/17
[44] What You Need to Know (and Don't) About the Aurora Vlunerability, Power Magazine, 9/1/2013

Because the U.S. grid is served by dozens of different electric utilities and different supervising operators, it is probably less susceptible to cyber-attack than if the grid were a national grid using uniform software and uniform equipment. Attempts to rationalize the grid and construct a so called smart grid may increase uniformity and centralization and thus increase susceptibility to cyber-attack.

After a grid collapse, restarting the grid is a laborious process. Only certain generating plants are *black start plants*, meaning that they can be started without needing outside electricity from the grid. A major power plant may need 50 or more megawatts of power to start up. The black start plants have onsite emergency power sufficient to start when the grid is down. To restart the grid the black start plants start first and they provide power via grid connections to allow other plants to start. Gradually the entire grid is bought to life and starts to shoulder the load. For this to work there has to be communications between the plants and the central operator. Circuit breakers and transmission lines have to work properly to move the power. This equipment may be damaged by an attack.

One approach to making the grid more resilient is *islanding*.[45] The idea is to bring up islands of electricity supported by one or a group of power stations. Ideally, such an island would never lose power in an attack, but might be disconnected from the grid by the loss of equipment or the failure of the grid outside of the island. The island should have communications, black start capability and control of the distribution network in its island area. Even if the island cannot fully service its power needs, giving power 8 hours per day on a rotating basis is infinitely better than a blackout. An islanding setup could keep sewage, water, traffic lights and gas stations running. With proper planning the financial system could be maintained so that credit cards would work.

---

[45] We use the term islanding, rather than microgrid. The microgrid term is associated with experimental and impractical schemes associated with renewable energy and batteries.

Diesel Generators to Provide Power for
Black Start at a Natual Gas Plant

The increasing domination of natural gas for generating electricity has implications for the possibility of islanding during an emergency. Just in time natural gas delivery often depends on a long chain, starting at gas wells or gas storage facilities, and continuing via pipeline, or even ships. Gas is transported in ships as a liquefied natural gas (LNG). A break anywhere in the chain stops delivery of gas. Some natural gas plants have backup oil tanks, but those fuel reserves are usually less substantial than found in the coal yard of a coal powered generating plant. Nuclear and hydro plants could also, in principle power, islands. The population in an island is infinitely better off with poor electrical service, that may include periodic cutoffs, as compared to having no electricity. In such a situation, critical services, such as water, sewage and fuel distribution, could be kept in operation. Without natural gas and with one or a few plants powering an island, it may not be possible to meet daily peaks by increasing and decreasing generation, but peaks can be managed by rotating blackouts. If a particular plant that could potentially power an island cannot be started because it needs grid power to start, then the island can't be enabled if the plant is down. This suggests that plants intended for islanding should be black start plants with a companion generator big enough to start the plant. For example, a turbine with an oil tank when substantial power is needed, or diesel generators for plants requiring less power to start. The emergency fuel would only be consumed when the main plant was being started.

When a plant trips offline because the external grid collapses, events may take place that complicate a subsequent restart. For example, the turbine shaft may bend slightly due to uneven cooling and require a long cool down before it can be restarted again. The hydrogen gas inside the generator, used to ensure low air friction, may automatically be purged for safety reasons and have to be reinstalled for restart. These problems could be avoided if the plant went into a standby condition, with the turbine still rotating but disconnected from the external grid load. Then if the local community could be configured as an island. The plant could quickly assume that load. During the standby condition the plant might provide the power needed within the plant, or the plant might go into a deep standby condition with power provided by black start generators to keep the plant ready for a quick start.

A 600-megawatt combined cycle natural gas plant, running 100 percent of the time, burns about $12,000 worth of fuel per hour. Or about $9 million per month. If fuel oil is used instead of natural gas the fuel will cost about 4 times as much assuming a cost of fuel of $2 per gallon, or $36 million a month. To store a month's supply of fuel on site would cost $36 million for 18 million gallons of fuel oil. A formidable tank farm would be required to store 18 million gallons of fuel oil. A tank 71-feet in diameter and 36-feet high holds one million gallons. Further the fuel oil deteriorates over time, so it has to be managed carefully.

On the other hand, a 600-megawatt coal generating plant would burn about 300 tons of coal per hour, costing about the same as natural gas or $12,000 an hour. A month's supply would be about 200,000 tons costing about $9 million. That amount coal could fit in a 10-20 acre yard depending on how it is stacked.

It is easy and not costly to keep several months of fuel on site for coal. For natural gas, investment in fuel storage infrastructure and fuel reserves is necessary. It is a crime against the safety of the American people that the Sierra Club is waging a politically inspired scare campaign[46] to close down coal plants. Although the Club may pretend that those plants are being replaced with wind and solar, they are actually replaced by natural gas plants. Wind and solar is a side show that replaces no grid infrastructure. Most gas plants have none or a few days of fuel reserves on site.

Although gas and coal are competitive in the cost of fuel, coal plants are more expensive to build. Cheap natural gas is recent due to the widespread adoption of fracking. The objective of the fracking is often to get valuable oil. Gas is a byproduct. If the cost of natural gas were to double, then coal would become competitive because the extra fuel cost for a natural gas plant would balance the extra capital cost for a coal plant. The price of natural gas may increase because the markets are expanding. It is being exported as liquefied natural gas (LNG). Natural gas can be used to fuel cars and trucks. It is considerably cheaper than gasoline or diesel. It is also possible that the price of oil could increase, making gasoline and diesel considerably more expensive and making natural gas more appealing as a substitute. Coal, on the other hand, is very plentiful and cheap. The main use of coal is for generating electricity.

The destruction of the electrical grid is a black swan event. A black swan event is an unusual event that is difficult to predict and that may have major importance. For example, another geomagnetic solar storm similar to the Carrington event of 1859 is likely to happen, but may not happen in the next 500 years. An EMP attack by North Korea or Iran may never take place, or it may come from the blue and be a surprise. Such an attack might have minor effect, or it might be devastating, resulting in the death of much of the population over a period of months. Protecting the electrical grid costs money. Both the government and the electrical utilities would rather ignore the problem, or convince themselves that there is no problem, rather than seriously deal with the problem.

In the case of crazy enemies, crazy defined as enemies driven by extremist ideology or ruled by mentally unstable dictators, political and military resolve is called for. If we keep pretending

---

46 The Sierra Club Beyond Coal campaign.

that these countries are going to become friendly if only we negotiate with them or give them money there is a distinct possibility that things will get worse. They will escalate threats with the intention of getting more money and more concessions. They may come to think of themselves as invincible and us as feeble and weak. If their collective connection with reality is lost, they may launch a nuclear–based EMP attack.

On the other hand, a few bombs dropped, or a few ships sunk, has a way of concentrating one's connection with reality. Force applied before events get out of hand is better than mutual assured destruction that is actually implemented. If you threaten your neighbor by pointing a gun and making verbal threats, you can expect that the police will arrive to arrest you for assault and confiscate your guns. If your neighbor threatens you, it is much more sensible to take the offense by calling in the police rather than building a bullet proof wall and sleeping each night in a bullet proof safe room. The same principle can be applied to relations between countries. Those countries that act like bullies and threaten others are best dealt with severely. Not only does that stop the threat, but it sets a fine example for others that might be tempted to go down the same road. These principles are very obvious, but politicians usually would rather kick the can down the road by pretending that bad behavior can be killed with kindness.

The People Needed to Maintain Critical Services

In an electrical supply emergency there is a great danger of chaos. One can imagine roads clogged by cars that have run out of fuel and grocery stores stripped bare by people spending their last reserves of folding money.

There are certain occupations that are critical for the survival of the national infrastructure in the case of a long blackout. If the police or military abandon their posts because they go home to take care of their families, the result will be chaos. Exactly the same applies to the workers that operate the electrical grid, sewer and water plants, fuel distribution, or the financial payments system. The electrical gird is an underappreciated vulnerability. We are unprepared for its long-term failure. We

have not even taken many simple steps to reduce the
vulnerability of the grid.

The Competitive Markets Movement

Traditionally, the companies that supplied electricity were regulated monopolies. State public utility commissions and the Federal Energy Regulatory Commission (FERC) extensively regulated the companies, telling them how to operate and how much to charge. In return the companies were given exclusive rights to supply electricity in their service areas and were allowed to use public right of ways for their power lines and equipment.

At some point the idea that the electric system should be based more on free market principles became popular. Academic theories of economics and game theory were used to figure out how the system should be reorganized. These theories depend on the assumption that the actors are behaving consistently with the assumptions underlying the economic theory. But the various actors, motivated by money, had the possibility of manipulating the "free" market to increase their own profits. The idea of a daily auction of electricity presents opportunities to create an artificial shortage and thus raise prices. A shortage can be created by shutting down plants for "maintenance," or by constricting transmission capacity, making it difficult for distant competitors to bring electricity to certain markets. The interests of the suppliers of electricity are to have a shortage of supply, thus driving up the prices. This is the opposite of the interests of the public in resilience and security of supply at reasonable prices. The interests of the public are served by having a plentiful supply of electricity.

The basic idea was to split the transportation and delivery of electricity from the generation of electricity. The utilities would still own the distribution network of power lines, but electricity would be supplied by independent power producers (IPP's). The IPP's would be entrepreneurial companies that built generating plants and competed with each other to supply electricity. In order to set the price an auction is held every day to determine which IPP's get to supply electricity the next day and how much they could charge for the electricity. The IPP's submit bids for supplying electricity. The bids would be ordered from low price to high price and accepted in order until enough electricity was bid to satisfy the projected need. The highest bid accepted would then set the rate for all suppliers. If a supplier bid too high, it would lose the right to supply electricity and its plants would sit idle. The result is that suppliers bid their marginal cost of providing electricity. That is the lowest price such that it is better sell electricity rather than have the plants be idle. For example, it makes no sense to sell electricity for less than the cost of the fuel used. It would be better to have the plant idle. If a supplier actually ends up selling electricity at the marginal price, that is a money losing proposition since none of the capital cost of the plant is being paid for, as well as other costs and profit. The supplier A is hoping or expecting that some other supplier, supplier B, is bidding higher, resulting in everyone, other than supplier B, getting paid more than their marginal cost.

It's fairly obvious how this can go wrong. If one power producer controls enough of the market, that producer can bid high and still win the right to sell electricity, because the other producers bidding lower cannot provide enough electricity. If no one producer is dominant enough, then several producers can work together, either secretly, or via an unspoken understanding, to raise the market price by bidding high.

The competitive market is far more complicated than the simplified discussion above. Other variables are where the electricity is delivered and when it is delivered. In many cases, there are auctions for capacity that is held in reserve.

In California, the California Independent System Operator (CAISO), a non-profit corporation, manages the auction system and the distribution of bulk electricity from various independent power producers. In the early 2000's the California system experienced turmoil and extremely high prices for electricity, at least partly caused by manipulation of the system for buying and selling electricity.

The Resilience Failure

It's difficult to say if the competitive markets have lowered the price of electricity in the dozen or so states that have adopted this scheme. Countering any savings due to competition is the increase in costs from increasing amounts of overpriced renewable energy.

The auction system encourages generators to cut corners and reduce overcapacity. Older plants that have higher cost structures are abandoned. New coal or nuclear plants are rare, instead natural gas plants are built because they have low capital costs and given the current price of natural gas the fuel is competitive with coal. But gas plants are dependent on just in time deliveries of natural gas. Gas plants lack resilience because they share the same weak link, the supply of gas via pipelines. If a gas pipeline fails or is overloaded, plants will have to shut down. Coal or nuclear plants can continue operating with fuel already on hand.

In New England gas pipeline delivery capacity is inadequate and power plants are behind residential users in priority for gas delivery. During a recent cold spell, some of the power plants had to switch from gas to oil stored in on-site oil tanks of limited capacity. If the cold spell had continued long enough the electricity supply would have been imperiled. (To make matters worse there is a trend toward using electrically powered pumping stations on gas pipelines, rather than gas powered pumps. That sets up a circular firing squad situation.)

New England uses imported Liquified Natural Gas (LNG) delivered to the Boston Area. Due to the Jones Act, American flagged LNG carriers must be used to transport LNG between American ports. But there are no American flagged LNG carriers, so the gas has to be purchased from countries like Russia.

Blackouts are extremely expensive for society because everyone stops working. Power companies are protected by law from having to pay the consequential damages from blackouts; thus, they don't have a proportionate incentive to make sure that blackouts don't happen. It is even worse than that because the power companies actively boycott moves that would protect the grid from blackouts. They are afraid that if they take action to lessen the chance of blackouts, they will be held responsible if a blackout does occur. For example, there is a protective device that can be installed to protect the critical transformers from destruction by solar storms or electromagnetic pulse. Only one power company installed the device on a few transformers and as a consequence was heavily, and out of public view, criticized by the power company community.

The Academic Villains

It seems that a lot of things that go wrong in our society are created by an over-reliance on academic theorizing. Global warming alarmism is entirely a construct of academic day dreaming. So is renewable energy. The idea of a competitive power market, with electricity sold using principles similar to the principles that would apply to sale of soybeans is very much the result of a theoretical construct built by academic economists. They start with the idea that the goal should be to minimize the cost of electric power. Minimizing cost is usual in economic theorizing. But, that idea is wrong because the most important goal should be to make electric power dependable. Even short blackouts are expensive. A long blackout would be a financial and human disaster. To make matters worse our enemies are working on ways to attack the electric grid.

Can the Country Regain its Sanity?

Renewable energy and its companion global warming alarmism have become a religion. There is a great danger that it will become an established religion forced on the people by the government and an elite establishment. Important believers include dignitaries such as Jerry Brown, the governor of California and Michael Bloomberg, billionaire and former mayor of New York. This is not a quiet religion. The believers don't meditate. This is an angry religion. The recruiters denounce those who don't believe and scream to the heavens that only they, the believers, know the truth. Everyone else needs to "listen to the science." Al Gore said, the non-believers in global warming are the type of people who think the Earth is flat and think the moon landing was faked in Hollywood. The climate scientist, James Hansen, wants to put people in on his enemies list in jail.

According to Omics International there are 180 journals, 183 conferences and 40 workshops dedicated exclusively to renewable energy.[47] The academic renewable industry is substantial and obviously, an obstacle to reform. If wind and

---

[47] https://www.omicsonline.org/renewable-energy-journals-conferences-list.php

solar go into the dust bin of history, the academic renewable energy industry would soon be headed in the same direction. So, naturally, the academic industry will lean toward supporting wind and solar and other forms of renewable energy. If renewable energy enjoyed the credibility it deserves, no one would be interested in reading journal articles about renewable energy.

Feed in tariffs, where utilities must pay retail price for rooftop solar electricity, are like passing a law that supermarkets have to buy my backyard apples at the same price they are selling apples. Further, I am entitled to simply walk into the supermarket, dump the apples and present a bill. If the supermarket has too many apples, it has to curtail its purchase of cheaper wholesale apples.

In New York, the pathetic governor, Andrew Cuomo, brags about banning fracking and closing down nuclear power plants. Cuomo wants New York to run on 50% renewable power by 2030. His democratic primary opponent, the loony left actress Cynthia Nixon, urges the enactment of the proposed *Climate and Community Protection Act.* That particular law would be better titled the *Climate and Community Economic Suicide Pact.* The law would endorse a comical list of fashionable, impracticable and utopian schemes, many involving renewable energy. Surely, most New Yorkers are not that concerned about the amount of renewable energy consumed. But apparently, there are enough strong believers in renewable energy so that the politicians feel it is necessary to cater to those believers.

The factual case against renewable energy is overwhelming. But, the opponents are mostly small think tanks and grass roots groups concerned about wind turbines. The grass roots opponents are often inspired by esthetic and environmental concerns rather than considerations of national energy policy. Very few politicians are strong opponents, probably due to the influence of the environmental organizations. That approximately 30 states have renewable portfolio standards is an indication of the strong political influence of the industry. The mass media is mainly characterized by mass ignorance. Major media outlets simply parrot industry propaganda.

There are other government subsidy programs that are retained due to special interest lobbying. For example, the sugar program that protects U.S. sugar producers with the result that sugar costs double the world price in the U.S. There is the corn ethanol program that mandates the production of corn ethanol as a gasoline additive, allegedly to prevent global warming, but actually to boost the price of corn and keep ethanol factories in business. That program affects Midwestern states important to the Republicans.

Unlike the sugar and ethanol programs, that only waste money, the renewable energy program is actually dangerous to the well-being of the country because it damages the resilience of the electrical grid.

Renewable energy has ideological support from environmental organizations and academic institutions. I doubt that any environmental organizations or think tanks support the sugar program. The sugar industry might have bought some academic support. One might think that the ethanol program would get environmental support since it supposedly fights global warming. But the Sierra Club does not like corn ethanol.[48]

If the sugar and ethanol program can survive with little support beyond self-interested lobbying, it is difficult to see how the renewable energy program, with more diversified support, can be terminated.

The best political attack on wind or solar may be to scream massive, seventy five percent, subsidy. Between the direct federal subsidies, tax equity financing and the sweetheart power purchase agreements an estimate of seventy five percent subsidy is reasonable. My calculation is that wind or solar costs about 7 cents/kWh at the plant fence and it is worth 2 cents in fuel saved. The difference between the cost of the electricity and its economic value is the subsidy. The subsidy is then $(7-2)/7 = 5/7$ths or 71%. To this can be added additional costs for increasing grid agility and the increase in cost of the gas turbine electricity due to lower capacity factor and lower thermal

---

[48] https://www.sierraclub.org/sierra/2017-1-january-february/grapple/are-we-stuck-corn-ethanol-forever-big-ag-would-us-think-so

efficiency associated with load following. Seventy five percent subsidy is probably conservative.

The advocates of renewable power will counter with a claim that fossil fuel is subsidized due to some modest tax arrangements. This is easily countered.[49] They will also claim that emission of CO_2 imposes costs on society. This can be countered with the benefits of CO_2, wind and solar being expensive ways of saving CO_2, and the dubious nature of the claims of global warming alarmism.

---

[49] http://www.api.org/news-policy-and-issues/taxes/#/?section=oil-and-natural-gas-companies-do-not-receive-subsidies

Appendix 1 – Levelized Cost of Energy

This appendix is a more elaborate discussion concerning the cost of various types of electricity. The Levelized Cost of Energy (LCOE) is used by various organizations as a way to compare the cost of various types of generating plants. Simply knowing the LCOE is not a complete measure of the value of a plant. In the real world, many other factors weigh heavily. For example, how fuel is transported to the plant, how electricity is carried to the users, and other more technical problems, such as the need for reactive power.

Formally, the LCOE is the cost of electricity such that the present value of the revenue streams less the present value of the cost streams, equals the present value of the cost of the project. That is, the gross profit is just enough to pay for the plant, or put it another way it is the cost of electricity when the plant operates at break even. The present value of a stream of payments assumes that payments in the future have a lower value now, discounted by a discount rate for each year into the future. We use a discount rate of 8%. It is not necessary to fully understand present value to follow the discussion here.

A simplified version of LCOE is used here. In the calculations, it is assumed that the generating plant has a contract to deliver electricity over a period of years at a fixed price. For example, deliver electricity for $80 per megawatt hour for 25 years. If that stream of revenue is just enough to pay for the building the plant and for the operating costs of the plant, then the $80 per megawatt hour is the LCOE. Of course, $80 per megawatt hour is 8-cents per kilowatt hour.

To further simplify the comparison of various types of generating plants we ignore minor expenses that would complicate the calculations. An example of a minor expense is property tax.

In the real world, the developer of a generating plant needs to make a profit, so the contract price generally must be higher than the LCOE, because the LCOE is a no-profit price. Roughly add 15% to our LCOE to get a real-world price including profit and minor expenses. Most discussions comparing power plants use the LCOE, no profit price, as do we.

For wind or solar plants the most critical factors are the capital cost, the capacity factor and the fixed maintenance costs. The capital cost is expressed as dollars per kilowatt of nameplate capacity. The nameplate capacity is the amount of power that can be produced when operating at full possible power, or at 100% capacity factor.

Wind Farm Example

For (on shore) wind plants, we use a capital cost of $1733 per kW of capacity. The capital cost is taken from the National Renewable Energy Laboratory[50] (NREL). The 36% capacity factor is typical of operating wind farms and close to the NREL mid suggestion. The fixed maintenance cost is taken as $52.50 per year per kW of capacity, also from NREL. We use middle values from NREL and adjust them by 5% to change 2015 dollars to 2018 dollars.

Using these numbers for a wind plant, a 100-megawatt wind plant would cost $1733 per kW of capacity to build, or $173.3 million. With a capacity factor of 36% it would, on average,

---

[50] The NREL annual technology baseline at https://atb.nrel.gov/

generate 36 megawatts, or 315,360 megawatt hours per year (8760 hours per year).

In order to compute the annual capital cost, we assume the plant is financed by a 25-year loan at 8% interest rate. Excel has a function PMT to calculate the annual payment, just as one would for a home mortgage:

=-PMT(.08,25,173300000) = $16,234,532

The annual payment on the plant mortgage is just over $16 million or $51.48 per megawatt hour. (16,234,532/315360)

For a wind farm, the capital cost is the greatest cost as no fuel is used.

The fixed maintenance cost of $52.50 per kW of capacity consists largely of labor costs, so we inflate that by 2.5% per year. To avoid having a different charge for maintenance each year, we levelize the maintenance cost by using an inflation adjustment factor of 1.273. If we multiply the $52.50 maintenance by 1.273 we get maintenance of $66.83 per year per kW. In other words, a maintenance charge of 52.50 escalating by 2.5% per year is equivalent to a charge of $66.83 the same every year for the 25 years. The total maintenance cost will be $6.683 million per year or $21.19 per megawatt hour. The total LCOE is the sum of the capital cost and the maintenance cost or $72.67 per megawatt hour.

Wind Farm Discussion

The estimate of 72.67 per megawatt hour is unsubsidized. Other authorities have lower estimates. The Lazard Company has an estimate of about $60 per megawatt hour. They use similar numbers to ours but include tax equity financing, really a government subsidy. NREL has a value of about $50 per megawatt hour but they include both tax equity financing and a much lower interest rate of 4.4%. Additional cost factors associated with wind are related to the fact that good wind is mainly in the Midwest. Our assumption of full financing at 8% interest would be unrealistic except for government policy guaranteeing market and pricing. It is questionable that wind turbines will actually last for 25 years considering that the 2.4 cent production tax credit expires in 10 years and a constant payment per megawatt hour becomes less valuable as time passes, due to inflation. In any case, it makes little difference to the overall analysis whether the LCOE is $5 or $7 per megawatt hour.

Natural Gas Plant Example

Calculating the LCOE for a natural gas plant is similar to Wind or Solar except that there is a fuel cost of about $22 per megawatt hour. We only consider a combined cycle natural gas plant – the most efficient type. A combined cycle plant uses a gas turbine as the first stage, then the hot exhaust of the gas turbine is used to make steam and drive a steam turbine. These plants are capable of extracting over 60% of the theoretical energy in the gas. Other types of fossil fuel plants don't get much over 40%. Although a combined cycle plant can run at near 100% capacity factor, in practice it is closer to 50% due to reduced usage at night and perhaps throttling up and down to follow wind or solar. Due to the reduced capacity factor, thermal efficiency also runs low, at about 50%. (There is no connection between 50% capacity factor and 50% thermal efficiency.)

The cost of natural gas over a 25-year period is difficult to predict. Gas is priced in dollars per million Btu (MMBtu). Currently the price is about $3.20 per MMBtu. 3420 Btu is the same amount of energy as a kilowatt hour. If the gas plant operates at 50% efficiency, the 6840 Btu is needed to generate one kWh. The fuel cost per kWh is then $3.20/(1000000/6840) = 2.2 cents per kWh. The price has been declining due to the growth of fracking. It is not clear if the price will increase or decrease in the longer term. If fracking becomes widespread in other countries, supply could greatly increase. On the other hand, exports of natural gas should tend to support the price. As a compromise, we assume a constant price in dollars. The construction cost of natural gas plants has also been declining The spreadsheet below calculates LCOE for wind, solar and natural gas. The Excel spreadsheet can be downloaded at:

dumbenergy.com/cost-of-electricity.html

	A	B	C	
	Wind Farm	**Solar Farm**	**Natural Gas**	**Formula**
Capacity factor	36%	19%	50%	
Nameplate Capacity (megawatts)	100	100	600	
Capital cosr per kW	$1,733	$1,208	$1,076	
Capital cost	$173,250,000	$120,750,000	$645,750,000	=C4*1000*C5
Plant lifetime (years)	25	25	25	
Discount rate	8%	8%	8%	
Inflation rate	2.50%	2.50%	2.50%	
Discount rate with inflation	5.366%	5.366%	5.366%	=(1+C8)/(1+C9)-1
Inflation adjustment factor	1.273	1.273	1.273	=PMT(C8,C7,PV(C10,C7,1))
Capital cost /year (millions)	$16,229,848.47	$11,311,712.57	$60,493,071.57	=-PMT(C8,C7,C6)
Electricity produced per year kilowatt hours	315,360,000	166,440,000	2,628,000,000	=C4*C3*24*365*1000
Capital cost / kilowatt hour	$0.051	$0.068	$0.023	=C12/C13
Plant thermal efficiency			50%	
Cost of natural gas per million Btu			$3.20	
Fuel cost per kilowatt hour			$0.022	=C16*(3420/1000000)/C15
Operation and Mainenance fixed cost / kW Capacity	$52.500	$12.600	$6.626	
Operation and maintenance per kilowatt hour			$0.002	
Total cost of electricity per kilowatt hour,	$0.0727	$0.0776	$0.0488	=C14+(C17+C19)+(C18*C4*1000*C11)/C13
Subsidy for wind per kilowatt hour- cost of wind electricity minus cost of fuel for gas	$0.051	$0.056		=A20-C17

Comparison of Cost Wind / Solar Farm and Combined Cycle Natural Gas Plant

Appendix 1

Other Cost Estimates

The Energy Information Administration (EIA) has published cost estimates for wind power that amount to 4.8 cents per kWh, exclusive of subsidies. That compares to my estimate of 6.84 cents. They use a capacity factor of 42% compared to my 36%. If the EIA used 36%, then its estimate would be closer to my estimate. It is not clear if the EIA is including a tax equity subsidy in their calculation.

Lazard gives a wind estimate of 6 cents per kWh. If you take tax equity financing out of their analysis, their estimate would be higher.

Capacity factor for wind turbines depends on the quality of the wind resource and the design of the turbine. The advocates of wind frequently assume a high capacity factor. If you really want more cost-effective power, the turbine needs to be bigger and taller. Wind is better higher up. If you can increase the turbine power output more than you increase the cost, cost-efficiency is increased.

Appendix 2 – Opponents of Renewable Energy and Sources

This is a list of organizations and publications critical of renewable energy.

Organization Websites

instituteforenergyresearch.org – Technical articles concerning renewable energy.
resilientsocieties.org – Leading authority on risks to the electric grid.
na-paw.org – North American Platform Against Windpower – lists of dozens of anti-wind organizations
WindAction.org – includes library of articles
Heartland.org
wiseenergy.org
wind-watch.org
ddowt.ca

Books

The Wind Farm Scam (Independent Minds) 1st Edition
by John Etherington

Paradise Destroyed: The Destruction of Rural Living by the Wind
Energy Scam by Gregg Hubner and Jamin Hubner

Wind Power Fraud by Charles Opalek

"THE PEOPLE'S WIND FARM" TURITEA NEW ZEALAND
CORRUPTION and FRAUD THE UNTOLD STORY by Paul Stichbury

The Solar Fraud: Why Solar Energy Won't Run the World by
Howard C. Hayden

Environmentalism Gone Mad: How a Sierra Club Activist and
Senior EPA Analyst Discovered a Radical Green Energy Fantasy
by Alan Carlin

The Little Green Book of Eco-Fascism: The Left's Plan to
Frighten Your Kids, Drive Up Energy Costs, and Hike Your Taxes!
By James Delingpole

Power Hungry: The Myths of "Green" Energy and the Real Fuels
of the Future by Robert Bryce

The False Promise of Green Energy by Roger E. Meiners and
Andrew Morris

Outside the Green Box: Rethinking Sustainable Development
Kindle Edition
by Steve Goreham

Energy Myths and Realities: Bringing Science to the Energy Policy
Debate by Vaclav Smil

Eco-imperialism: Green Power, Black Death by Paul Driessen

Appendix 2

Copyright, Disclaimer

Made in the USA
Middletown, DE
31 August 2018